Living Authentically Through Color

For Autistic Women+ (and other curious minds)

Shannon Hilscher,
Confetti Dreamer

Living Authentically Through Color: For Autistic Women+ (and other curious minds)

© Copyright 2024 Confetti Dream Publishing, LLC

All rights reserved. No part of this publication may be reproduced, distributed or transmitted in any form or by any means, including photocopying, recording, or other electronic or mechanical methods, without the prior written permission of the publisher, except in the case of brief quotations embodied in critical articles or reviews and certain other noncommercial uses permitted by copyright law.

Although the author and publisher have made every effort to ensure that the information in this book was correct at press time, the author and publisher do not assume and hereby disclaim any liability to any party for any loss, damage, or disruption caused by errors or omissions, whether such errors or omissions result from negligence, accident, or any other cause.

At the time of publication, all printed URLs printed in the book were accurate and active. Not responsible for the accessibility of any website.

Neither the author nor the publisher assumes any responsibility or liability whatsoever on behalf of the consumer or reader of this material. Any perceived slight of any individual or organization is purely unintentional.

The resources in this book are provided for informational purposes only and should not be used to replace the specialized training and professional judgment of a health care or mental health care professional.

Neither the author nor the publisher can be held responsible for the use of the information provided within this book. Please always consult a trained professional before making any decision regarding treatment of yourself or others.

Artificial intelligence (AI) was not used to write this book. Adobe Firefly was used to generate a few images, noted in context.

For more information, email contact@confettidreamers.com.

ISBN: 978-1-73460-7-437 (paperback)
ISBN: 9781-73460-7-451 (hardcover)
ISBN: 978-1-73460-7-444 (ebook)

Library of Congress Control Number: 2024917261

VIDEO INTRODUCTION

Watch this short video for a quick explanation of the two-part structure of this book and how to use the free resources to guide your journey:

Part 1: Our Colored World
Part 2: Autism in Women+

ConfettiDreamers.com/Video
ConfettiDreamers.com/Color
ConfettiDreamers.com/Autism

Dedication

To Jerome, my husband and rock: Thank you for believing in me. You have been incredibly patient, flexible, and supportive over the past four years. Thank you for entertaining my colorful dreams to share with others. *Wonder powers, activate!*

To Ellie: I'm so proud of you for pursuing a diagnosis long before it was even on my radar. You are the reason I started this journey after sharing the Facebook group with me and piquing my interest. You have taught me so much about embracing Autism as a gift, and I am forever grateful. I hope our story helps others embrace their authentic (Autistic) selves earlier in life.

To Ellie and Grace: After years of masking, thank you for helping and humoring me on my journey to find my authentic self. I am incredibly proud of both of you. You have taught me even more about diversity, inclusion, and the importance of standing up for those who need a voice.

To my mom, Dianne: Thank you for being you. I have gained so much from you: creativity, kindness, resourcefulness, resilience, and conviction. You made it okay to talk about mental health. Your emotional support (and Bob's) played a key role in giving me the courage to take this journey of self-discovery. I can't wait to see how you continue to express yourself through color.

To my hysterical WBCA girls (Carla, Rachel, and Kolette): Our trips to Minnesota are forever etched into my brain. It was the first group experience as an adult that I embraced as my authentic, child-like self. My belly aches just thinking about all the laughter; so much fun!

To Carla, my person: You get me. When you say I make you laugh, think, or feel inspired, all I can say is, "ditto." Thank you for always graciously sharing your kindness, compliments, and words of encouragement. Without your words, *Confetti Dreamers* may have remained an idea. I am forever grateful to you. Your girls are so lucky to have you as their mom.

To Jackie: I absolutely adore your willingness to have a patchwork of friends that includes me. Thank you for being a loyal friend and biking partner despite how different we are.

To Megan: Thank you for finding me after thirty-four years. You are the epitome of a *confetti dreamer.*

To all women+ who are trying to find their authentic selves. As a sign of inclusivity and belonging, the plus (+) sign in the title and throughout this book extends this invitation to people identify as women—plus (+) people who identify as trans, non-binary, gender fluid, or agender.

Contents

Prologue xi
   Why I Studied Color xi
   Color Is a Basic Human Need xii
   Your Invitation xiii
      An exploration into color as a special interest xiii
      A surprise journey into the colorful world of Autism xiv
      Confetti Dreamers xv

Part One | Our Colored World | An Exploration into Color as a Special Interest

Chapter 1 | What Is Color? 3
   To See Color, You Must Have Light (and Sight) 3
   Subtractive Color or Additive Color 4
   A Note about Color Blindness 5

Chapter 2 | Color Theory Models 6
   Red, Yellow, Blue (RYB) = Traditional Primaries 7
   Cyan, Magenta, Yellow (CMY) = Modern Primaries 7
   Red, Green, Blue (RGB) = Mixing of Light 7

Chapter 3 | Subtractive Color Models (Traditional vs. Modern)
| The Mixing of Colorants 8
   Pigments 8
   Dyes 9
   Timeline of Colored Pigments and Dyes 10

- Subtractive Primary Colors 11

Chapter 4 | Traditional RYB Primaries on the Color Wheel 13
- RYB Color Wheel (Front) 14
- RYB Color Wheel (Back) 15
- RYB Color Definitions 16
- Color Variations 17

Chapter 5 | Traditional RYB Primaries Not on the Color Wheel 20
- Equal Parts 20
- Blacks 21
- Whites 22
- Grays 23
- Browns 23
- Skin Tones 24

Chapter 6 | Traditional RYB Primaries | Relationships on the Color Wheel 27
- Color Formulas for Harmonious Color Schemes 28
- Using Color Formulas 36

Chapter 7 | Modern CMY Primaries on the Color Wheel 38
- CMY Color Wheel (Front) 41
- CMY Color Wheel (Back) 42
- CMY Color Definitions 43
- Color Variations 43
- CMYK System for Printers 44

Chapter 8 | Modern CMY Primaries| Relationships on the Color Wheel ... 50
- Color Formulas for Harmonious Color Schemes 51
- Visual Communication 57

Chapter 9 | RGB Additive Primary Colors | The Mixing of Light 59
- Light Waves of Color: Primary and Secondary Colors 60
- Colors on a Screen 63

Chapter 10 | The Best Color Model for Printing 74
- File Formats for Printing 74
- Color Theory Models (revisited) 75
- An Amazing World of Printed Color 76

Chapter 11 | Color Psychology 78
- A Brand's Color Story 78
- Confetti Dreamers 80

Chapter 12 | Everything (Anything) on a Spectrum 82
- Familiar Spectrums 83

    Other Spectrums 84
Chapter 13 | Spectrums of Color Meanings 86
Chapter 14 | Cultural Color Meanings 94
Chapter 15 | Rainbows 96
    Symbolism 96
    Embrace the Rainbow as 'More Than' 97

Part Two | An Enlightening Adventure into the World of Neurodiversity and Autism

Chapter 16 | Color and Neurodiversity 101
    What Color Are You? 103
    What Color Is Your Authentic Self? 103
    Embrace Your True Colors 105
    Neurodiversity 105
    The Spectrum of Neurodiversity 107
Chapter 17 | Autism 109
    Early Days of Autism 109
    Why Autistic Women+? 110
    Autism in Women+ 112
    Masking 112
    The Autism Spectrum | Many Visual Representations 113
    Autistic Traits 119
    Some Co-occurring Conditions 121
Chapter 18 | Signs of Stress and Its Effects 124
    Effects of Stress 124
    The Color of Stress 125
    Stress-related Terminology 126
Chapter 19 | Seeing the Light, Feeling the Hope 131
    Radiant Colors of Positivity 133
    Glimmers 134
    Coping with Triggers 134
    Stimming 142
    Pacing 144
Chapter 20 | Should You Get a Diagnosis? 146
    Self-Discovery Tools 147
    Getting a Diagnosis 149

Diagnostic Resources 150
What to Expect When You're Expecting a Formal Diagnosis 154
What Next? 154
Accommodations 155
Likely Pushback 156
When Sharing: I'm Autistic 157
Adapting to the New You: Plan or Wing It 158

Chapter 21 | Maslow's Hierarchy of Needs in Color 161
Physiological Needs 162
Safety Needs 163
Love and Belonging 164
Esteem 165
Self-Actualization 166
What Are Your True Colors? 167
Side Note: It's No Accident 168
A Serendipitous Moment in My Journey 169

Epilogue 171
Your Invitation 171

Books About Color 173
References for Part One | Color 175
Digital Color Tools 179
References for Part Two | Autism Spectrum Disorder 181
Appendix A. Color Models Quick Reference Guide 189
Appendix B. HEX Code Explanation 191
Acknowledgements 193
Spread the News! 195
Check Out My Other Book 197
An Adventure into Our Colored World: The Before and After 197
Public Service Announcement (PSA) 199
Index 201

Prologue

Vibrant color sparks a sense of delightful contentment that feeds my soul with a creative charge. While I can't trace my passion for color to a love-at-first-sight memory or experience, it's part of my soul. I respond to color the way a chocolate fanatic swoons over a cascading fountain of delectably smooth chocolate. It takes me to my happy place of complete bliss.

I love to immerse myself in vivid colors, whether it's mixing and matching delightful paint swatches like a kid in a candy shop, wrapping myself in a silky Mexican shawl, or feasting my eyes on intriguing quilt patterns. Color is magical.

Why I Studied Color

Board books on color are plentiful for babies and toddlers, but I was curious to see what was available for adults. When I started my 'color book' journey, I immersed myself in what was readily available at my public library. Most books start by explaining the history and science of color—Isaac Newton's experiments with prisms and the discovery of 'Roy G. Biv.' The color wheel then connects us to terms from childhood, like primary and secondary colors. After covering basic terminology, color then becomes the framework for a deeper dive into the glorious, multifaceted science and theory of color, applying it to an infinite list of topics.

Color Is a Basic Human Need

Perhaps color is everywhere because it is a "basic human need" (Eckstut, 2013). This may sound overdramatic. But is it?

Color-coded signs keep us safe. Dressing in our favorite colors makes us happy. Choosing a color palette for our home expresses our personality. Creating art or enjoying someone else's masterpiece can soothe or inspire.

During my immersive journey, it struck me: color is threaded throughout Maslow's Hierarchy of Needs. Color IS life. Color IS a basic human need.

In 1954, psychologist Abraham Maslow created this hierarchical model to explain motivations for human behavior. This first image captures a typical representation.

Maslow's Hierarchy of Needs

Self-actualization
desire to become the most that one can be

Esteem
respect, self-esteem, status, recognition, strength, freedom

Love and belonging
friendship, intimacy, family, sense of connection

Safety needs
personal security, employment, resources, health, property

Physiological needs
air, water, food, shelter, sleep, clothing, reproduction

© Plateresca 2017[1]

---

[1] https://www.istockphoto.com/portfolio/Plateresca?mediatype=illustration

Here is my interpretation of Maslow's Hierarchy of Needs in the context of color.

Maslow's Hierarchy of Needs in Color

© Confetti Dream Publishing, LLC 2024

Your Invitation

Come along with me on a two-part journey into our colored world:

1. An exploration into color as a special interest.
2. A surprise journey into the colorful world of Autism.

An exploration into color as a special interest

A special interest is like a hobby. For some, having one or two hobbies is enough to fuel their soul. For others, their hobbies fluctuate—adding, subtracting, multiplying, and dividing. For me, color has multiplied into a passion with numerous subsets.

In the first section of this book, I share some of what I learned about color on my journey—the science of color, the two types of subtractive primary colors, additive primary colors (the mixing of light), color theory, color psychology, and the symbolism of color. The term 'spectrum' is woven throughout as a tool to show a range of—well, just about anything.

A surprise journey into the colorful world of Autism

The second half of this book is about neurodiversity, specifically Autism and its presentation in women+.

For starters, what is neurodiversity?

Here are a couple definitions from the Autistic community.

From the organization, Reframing Autism:

Neurodiversity is "a biological fact that there exists a diversity of human minds; [a] term coined by Judy Singer to denote the infinite variation in neurocognitive functioning within the species."

From Sonny Jane Wise (livedexperienceeducator.com, 2024):

"Neurodiversity refers to the diversity of human minds and all the unique and different ways that people can exist, think, act, process, feel, and function."

What's the connection between color and neurodiversity?
They both relate to spectrums.

In a way, e-v-e-r-y-t-h-i-n-g is on a spectrum—a scale or a range. When I think of spectrums, the two that most frequently come to mind are the color spectrum and the Autism spectrum. Because these two spectrums have greatly impacted my perspective of the world, the relationship between them and the importance of learning more about them are among my passions.

Throughout my life, I have been an observer—watching others enjoy life in social (sometimes highly unpredictable) settings. Don't get me wrong; I live a fulfilling life and push myself out of my comfort zone with each sunrise. However, as a result of the COVID-19 pandemic (in the year 2020+), which has impacted people in ways we are just now starting to understand, I discovered a private Facebook group, **Autistic Women+ Living Authentically**, that connected me with a wonderful, diverse group of Autistic people (Autists) who identify across the colorful spectrum of gender. Given that I (now) identify as an Autistic woman, this group has allowed me to uncover an amazing sense of belonging, peace, and purpose where people are 'seen,' acknowledged, and validated within a community of neurodivergent individuals. I invite you to read Part Two to learn about Autism and how it presents in women. Even if this is not your identity, my hope is to inspire you to live your best life.

Confetti Dreamers

I now think of myself as a **confetti dreamer**—that is, **someone who lives authentically in color**. I long for you to embrace the confetti dreamer in you, too.

© Confetti Dream Publishing, LLC 2024

Confetti Dreamer

Color
Outside
Normalcy.
Forever
Embrace
Talents.
Tickle
Inspiration.

Do
Real.
Evolve
Authentically.
Marvel
Enthusiastically.
Repeat.

© Confetti Dream Publishing, LLC 2024

Part One

Our Colored World | An Exploration into Color as a Special Interest

Chapter 1

What Is Color?

Color is perception.

Although color is based on the science of light waves, everyone's brain is unique. This means how our brains perceive color is also unique—like a fingerprint. The way you see, interpret, and react to color is personal.

To See Color, You Must Have Light (and Sight)

As a child, I distinctly remember touring a cave. One of the experiences they offered was a pitch-black tunnel. They turned off all lights and flashlights. For about thirty seconds, there was no light, no hue—just complete and utter lack of color.

At the time, I thought it was a silly demonstration because my room was always dark at bedtime, but this was a new level of darkness—and that was the point.

Subtractive Color or Additive Color

Our eyes see light either **reflected from an object** or from a **light source** (Konstantinovsky and Bowie, 2023).

This distinction is important because each type of light involves its own color theory:

- **Subtractive** color mixing relates to the mixing of pigments and dyes. The light waves that reflect from a colored object (e.g., a blue crayon) result in the color you see (blue).
- **Additive** color mixing is the mixing of light waves. The light comes from a light source (e.g., a blue light bulb).

Why two color theories?

When mixing colored pigments and dyes, the perceived results are different from the results of mixing colored light.

With both theories, seeing color depends on the anatomy of our eyes, specifically the three types of cone photoreceptors that are sensitive to red, green, and blue light.

When light shines on an object, some colors bounce off and some are absorbed. Our eyes, with the help of our brain, see the colors that bounce off. Our cone photoreceptors then interpret the amounts of light.

You **can see** colors that reflect or bounce off.

You **cannot see** colors that are absorbed.[2]

---

[2] © "Outline eye vector outline" by Canva creator thanhloc123 2024

A Note about Color Blindness

I wrote this book from the perspective of someone who can see a wonderful array of vivid colors. It is important to acknowledge color blindness, though, because it impacts 350 million people worldwide; this is equivalent to the population of the United States. Although there is no cure for colorblindness, there are special glasses to help improve color vision (EnChroma, 2024).

> What causes color blindness?
>
> The cone photoreceptors in our eyes help our brain make sense of the microvariations in color. Color blindness occurs when the red and green cones overlap, making it difficult for the brain to distinguish between red and green shades of color.

Special lenses, such as EnChroma lenses, are designed to filter light and alleviate the overlap of cones, expanding the range of color detection so it's more accurate. If you haven't seen it, take a few minutes to search the internet for "glasses for colorblind video" or "Top 15 Moments People Seeing Color." Watching someone who is colorblind see color for the first time is amazing. Their reactions are emotional, jaw-dropping, and often full of happy tears as they literally soak in a more vibrant world for the first time.

If you think you might be color blind, search the internet for "color blind tests" or "Ishihara color plates." For example, if you cannot see the "12" in the following image, you may be colorblind.[3]

Ishihara_1.svg by Nicoguaro is marked with CC0_1.0.

---

[3] https://commons.wikimedia.org/w/index.php?curid=47050887 by https://commons.wikimedia.org/wiki/User:Nicoguaro is marked with https://creativecommons.org/publicdomain/zero/1.0/deed.en?ref=openverse

Chapter 2

Color Theory Models

If you search for "What is color theory?" on the internet, you will get a variety of answers. Color theory is:

- a guide to color meaning
- a logical structure for color
- a playbook for communicating with your audience
- the science and art of using color
- a way to explain how humans perceive color
- a variety of design principles that apply to the context and use of color
- a study of how colors work together and affect our emotions and perceptions

In other words, color theory is multifaceted, layered, and quite complex; however, it also includes models and tools to simplify important information. These tools provide a framework for experimentation.

These three color models are covered in this book.

Red, Yellow, Blue (RYB) = Traditional Primaries

Traditional primaries—Red, Yellow, Blue (RYB) —are **subtractive** primary colors related to the mixing of pigments and dyes in a medium (e.g., paint). These are also called **artist's primaries.**

Cyan, Magenta, Yellow (CMY) = Modern Primaries

Modern primaries—Cyan, Magenta, Yellow (CMY)—are **subtractive** primary colors related to the mixing of pigments and dyes in a medium (e.g., ink). These are also referred to as **printer's primaries.**

Red, Green, Blue (RGB) = Mixing of Light

RGB Color Model | Red, Green, Blue | These are additive primary colors related to the mixing of light.

As you read about these color theory models, you may find it helpful to reference **Appendix A. Color Theory Models Quick Reference Guide.**

Chapter 3

Subtractive Color Models (Traditional vs. Modern) | The Mixing of Colorants

Pigments and dyes are colorants used to add color to, or change the visual appearance of, a physical material.

Pigments

Pigments are "solid organic or inorganic compounds that exhibit color in their solid form" (Pylam Dyes, 2023). Pigments are finely ground powders mixed with a thick liquid, paste, or solid that can be applied as color to an object. The pigment particles *physically* bind or stick to the object.

Like mud in water, pigments are *insoluble*, meaning they do not dissolve. Instead, the dirt particles (pigments) *suspend* in the medium. If you let a cup of muddy water sit long enough, the larger dirt particles (pigments) sink to the bottom, eventually leaving clear water at the top. This type of liquid mixture is called a *suspension*.

Historically, pigments were derived from naturally occurring substances—**natural pigments**. Over time, pigments were created through chemical processes in labs and factories. These **synthetic pigments** can be brighter, more durable, and more cost-effective to produce compared to natural pigments.

Some common uses of pigments include artist's paints (watercolor, oils, acrylics, and gouache), polishes, stains, house paints, foods, drugs, cosmetics, coatings, plastics, resins, and rubber.

Dyes

Simplified, **dyes** are colored chemicals that are liquid or *soluble*, meaning they are easily dissolvable in water, **and** they chemically bind to the object or material they are coloring.

Unlike pigments in *suspensions*, dyes work in *solutions*. For comparison, when a teaspoon of sugar is mixed with a cup of water, the sugar completely *dissolves*. The sugar (*solute*) dissolves in the water (*solvent*) to create a *solution* (not a *suspension*). If left covered to avoid evaporation, the sugar water will **not** separate. This is also true for liquid dyes. They are solutions, meaning the dye doesn't separate from the solvent.

Dyes used to dye fabrics can come from nature (berries, bark, leaves, and roots); however, most dyes used today are **synthetic** (manufactured). Dyes are classified by type, with some common uses including textiles, paper products, hair dye, cleaning products, inks, waxes, and polishes.

We have more colors available at our fingertips than ever before, yet we're still searching for more. Experimentation and advancements in the use of pigments and dyes continue today. The following timeline[4] shows the evolution of colored pigments and dyes. Recent additions demonstrate that scientists are still making discoveries on the quest for brighter colors.

---

[4] © "Colorful Modern Business Chronology Timeline Infographic" by Canva creator Yadira Inza 2024

Timeline of Colored Pigments and Dyes

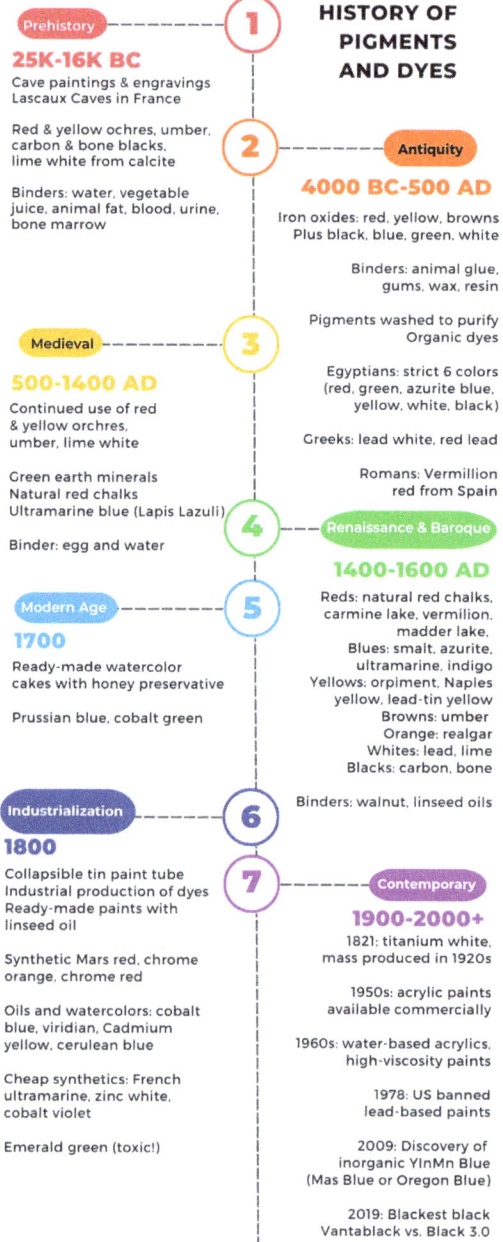

Subtractive Primary Colors

Subtractive **primary colors** are made from **reflected** light. (●●●) [5]

The sensation of color is produced when a surface absorbs all the light wavelengths and frequencies except those the eyes perceive—that is, the absorbed light waves are 'subtracted' from what is visible.

The color you see is based on the chemical makeup of the object and its reflection of light as a color. All objects, whether naturally formed or not, have physical and chemical properties that impact which color light waves are absorbed (not visible) and which ones are reflected (visible).

If you color an object, you alter the physical and/or chemical properties of it—and, therefore, change what color light waves are absorbed and reflected (Adams, 2017).

Examples:

- Stain a piece of wood
- Paint on canvas
- Dye a t-shirt
- Draw with chalk on a sidewalk

Shockingly, there are two types of **subtractive primary colors**, each with their own color coding.

- **Traditional primaries** = red, yellow, blue (RYB)
    o The 'simple' primary colors you learned as a child
    o Equal parts R + Y + B = brown (*sometimes* to the black)
- **Modern primaries** = cyan, magenta, and yellow (CMY)
    o Arguably, a more complete set
    o Equal parts C + M + Y = (almost) black
    o Equal parts C + M + Y + black = (true) black

The traditional **RYB primaries** were mostly sufficient until there was a need for printing in color. Modern **CMY primaries** were first used in the 1890s

---

[5] Whenever you see these three dots (●●●), it means "more details to come later."

for printing. These CMY primaries became the standard for printing in the 1940s because it has a much wider range, or gamut, of colors.

Let's look at the traditional primaries first, since it most likely aligns with your first lessons on color.

Chapter 4

Traditional RYB Primaries on the Color Wheel

As a starting point for understanding color, my artist friends recommended color wheels from The Color Wheel Company. A color wheel is a visual representation of color used by both amateurs and professionals to "promote understanding of color theory, color relationships, and color mixing" (colorwheelco.com). Using a color wheel can help you create harmonious art by experimenting with color mixing and color formulas.

RYB Color Wheel (Front)

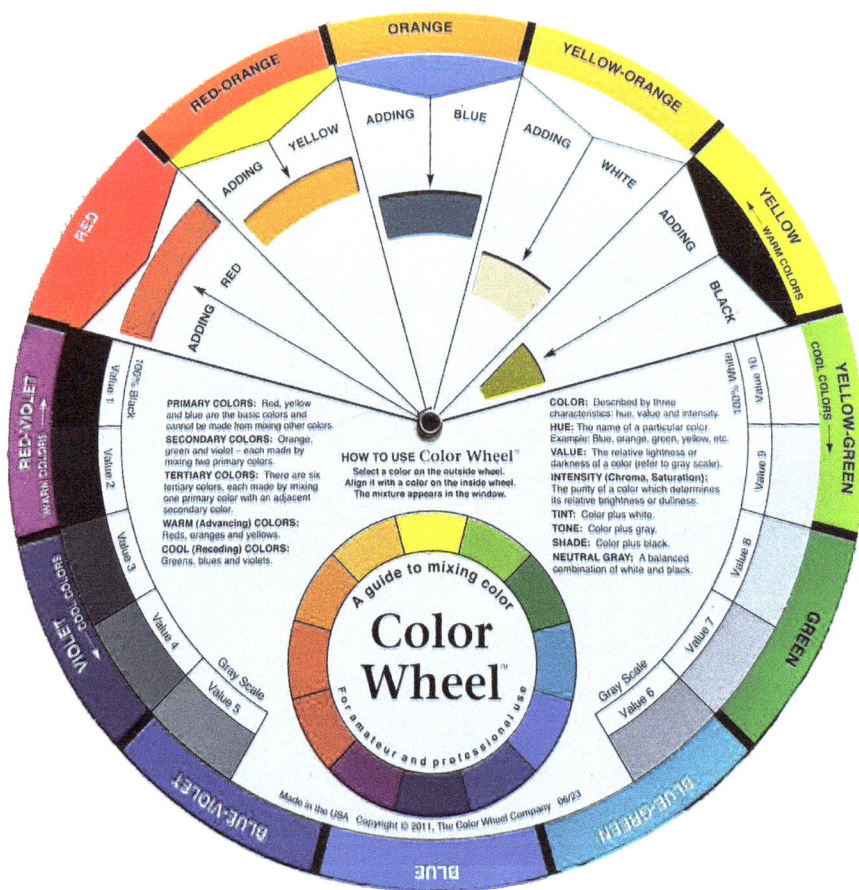

RYB Color Wheel (Back)

© The Color Wheel Company™ 2024

Used with permission by The Color Wheel Company, PO Box 130, Philomath, OR 97370.

If you love the images, these color wheels can be ordered directly online from The Color Wheel Company.[6]

---

6   https://colorwheelco.com/

How do you use the color wheel?

If you select a color on the outside wheel and align it with a color on the inside wheel, the mixture appears in the window.

RYB Color Definitions

These definitions are primarily from The Color Wheel Company, with some additional insights I found on my journey. Refer to the images to find the following colors.

Primary colors:

- Cannot be made from mixing other colors
- Red, yellow, and blue (RYB)

Secondary colors:

- Each made by mixing two primary colors:
    - Red + Yellow = Orange (R + Y = O)
    - Yellow + Blue = Green (Y + B = G)
    - Blue + Red = Violet (B + R = V)

Tertiary colors:

- Six colors, each made by mixing one primary with an adjacent secondary color:
    - Red + Violet = **Red-violet**
    - Red + Orange = **Red-orange**

- Yellow + Orange = **Yellow-orange**
- Yellow + Green = **Yellow-green**
- Blue + Green = **Blue-green**
- Blue + Violet = **Blue-violet**

Color Variations

Four **qualities** of color—hue, intensity, value, and temperature—can be used to create color variations.

Hue is the name of a particular color (another name for color).

Hue includes:

- The purest, brightest color
- Colors located in the outer ring of the color wheel
- The correlating color on the rainbow spectrum
- No white or black when fully saturated

Intensity is also called chroma or saturation.

Intensity is the purity of a color, which determines its brightness (vividness) or dullness:

- Vibrant colors are saturated. Color from a paint tube is about as vivid as it can be in paint form.
- Dull colors are desaturated. Life would be too stimulating without these colors.

To make a color duller (less vivid), you can neutralize it by mixing its complementary color. This moves the color to a brownish or grayish tone. (●●●)

- Example: Red + Green = Brown
- Zero saturation of any hue = Gray

As you mix subtractive primary colors (traditional or modern), the resulting color becomes less pure because more light waves are being absorbed (subtracted). Eventually, the resulting color is perceived as a dark muddy color.

For **vibrant (saturated)** colors, it is better to use a single pigment—like the color straight out of the tube—rather than mixing several together to achieve a similar color.

Why? Because each color you use in your mixture absorbs more available light wavelengths, resulting in dull or murky colors.

Value is the relative lightness or darkness of a color. When trying to recreate reality, value is critically important.

Value includes:

- **Shades:** Color + black to deepen the value
    - Examples: Navy is a shade of blue, and maroon is a shade of red.
- **Tints:** Color + white to lighten the value
    - Example: Pink is a high value red.
- **Tones:** Color + gray to create tonal colors
    - Tinting and shading a color creates tonal colors for a contrasting range of values.

A helpful tool for determining value is a **Gray Scale & Value Finder**. The tool is divided into ten graduated steps. By comparing the gray scale to your color, you can determine its specific value and intensity. Knowing the value of a color will aid in correctly and efficiently mixing and matching colors.

Temperature relates to how warm or cool the color is:

- Warm colors (advancing colors)
    - Reds, oranges, yellows
    - Think sunshine
- Cool colors (receding colors)
    - Greens, blues, violets
    - Think calm and refreshing

Other variations listed on the color wheel:

- **Key Color:** Predominant color in a color scheme of a painting or other creative project
- **Neutral Gray:** A balanced combination of white and black

The next chapter explains white, black, gray, and brown in relation to the traditional color wheel.

Chapter 5

Traditional RYB Primaries Not on the Color Wheel

The Color Wheel mentions whites, blacks, and grays in the context of value but doesn't address browns. Because these colors are critical when creating lifelike art, let's take a closer look.

Equal Parts

When color mixing, you may see the phrase, "mix equal amounts of each color." This does not mean equal amounts of paint, such as 50 percent red and 50 percent yellow.

Instead, "using equal parts" means applying the same measuring method for each color when mixing a ratio of colors. The quantity of paint needed for your project influences your unit of measurement.

- For small quantities, you might measure in drops, blobs of approximately the same size, or teaspoons.
  - 2 drops violet + 3 drops blue
- If precision is important, you might place a lightweight plate on your kitchen scale and zero out the plate's weight before adding the exact proportion in grams. This is helpful if you need to reproduce the exact same color again.
  - 0.5 gram of violet + 1 gram of blue

One of the most effective ways for this principle to 'click' is to experiment with color mixing. Lisa Solomon's book, *A Field Guide to Color: A Watercolor Workbook*, provides a framework for that very purpose in the context of watercolor paints. There are also many videos and books on color mixing in other mediums.

Blacks

A curious thing, black is used to shade a hue and deepen its value. Most artists, however, rarely use black from a tube.

Really? Why not?

Because it can be too much. It feels out of place or jarring.

Instead, artists often mix colors from their palette, excluding white, to create a harmonious black-like color used for shading (Dewey, 2017). Interesting.

Alternatives for mixing **dark colors** without using black from a tube:

- Use a primary + a secondary:
  - Yellow + purple
  - Blue + orange
  - Red + green
- Use brown + blue
- Use brown + blue + red

Remember, a black object absorbs all color equally and reflects no color. Therefore, it **subtracts** *all colored light waves from being visible. For a black that leans to the green, all color is absorbed equally except for certain green light waves.*

Some scientists think black is not a color; rather, it is the absence of color because no visible light reaches the eye. My book, *The Unexpected Adventure That Changed My World*, describes black as a mysterious color, surprisingly full of movement because it has absorbed all other colors and needs to express the pent-up energy.

Whites

Many novice painters start adding whites too early in the process. Whites should be used sparingly and later in the painting process to highlight and convey light. This is because white lightens the value and creates tints.

When it comes to selecting a white, there are more than 150,000 options to choose from. Some whites are warm, while others are cool. If you're painting a room in white, search for trends and recommendations from interior designers or ask for assistance at a store specializing in paints. Several factors, such as lighting, sheen, and contrasting wall color, can impact your final result.

If working with acrylics, there are three common whites (Dewey, 2019):

- Most common white = titanium white
    - has strong tinting quality
    - makes the mixed-in color opaque
    - is a smooth, cooler white
    - is a relatively new white (twentieth century)
- Zinc white
    - is slightly warmer than titanium white
    - is not quite as opaque
    - should be avoided with thick paint
    - is best used sparingly; it can damage (delaminate) your paint
    - is an older white (nineteenth century)
- Mixing white
    - does not tint as dramatically
    - is a chalky, cold white
    - keeps some saturation while lightening values
    - is a warmer white with some grit (not as smooth)

Grays

When you combine white and black, you get neutral grays. But, of course, the options don't end there.

If you want a "yummy gray," as described by artist Carol A. McIntyre (2021), be prepared to have some fun experimenting. In her article, "Why is Mixing Gray so Important for Painters?," McIntyre walks you through the steps and provides pictures for reference.

Here's an overly simplified summary:

1. Mix red, blue, and yellow (plus a little white) = 'lifeless' gray.
2. Add a little blue to the result of 1 = blue-gray.
3. Add a little red to the result of 2 = lavender-gray.
4. Add a little more red to the result of 3 = rose-gray.
5. Add yellow to the result of 4 = tan-gray.
6. Add yellow + blue to the result of 5 = green-gray.

To determine an effective contrasting color that pops with these grays, use with the complementary (opposite) color of the gray's bias color:

- Use orange with blue-gray because blue and orange are complements.
- Use yellow with lavender-gray.
- Use green with rose-gray.
- Use purple with tan/yellow-gray.
- Use red with green-gray.

Who would've thought grays could be so fun!

Browns

Although brown is not on the default color wheel of highly saturated hues, if you darken (desaturate) the color wheel, the orange and dark orange sections become brown. Neat!

You can mix a little black with orange to get brown, or you can mix complementary colors to get brown (Clamp, 2023). Examples:

- Orange + some blue
- Yellow + violet
- Red + green

Skin Tones

It can be challenging to paint or color realistic skin tones. To understand how to grow your skills in this area, let's look at the science of skin tones.

Skin tones in real life vary greatly because of several factors (Boissonnault, 2005):

- Melanocytes, found deep in the skin, contain **melanin**, which are **brown** granules that impact skin color and protect the skin.
- **Carotene**, found in fat tissue is a **yellowish** color (e.g., palms and feet).
- Local **blood** flow and oxygenated **hemoglobin** produces a **reddish** color.

These factors result in a wonderfully diverse spectrum of skin tones, which has greatly influenced the color industry. For example, the multi-billion-dollar makeup industry prides itself on color-matching concealer and foundation products.

Since many skin colors have brown undertones due to melanin, you can use the formulas for mixing browns as a starting point for creating skin tones with paint.

In 2020, Crayola® launched its "Colors of the World" skin tones in three main shades of **almond**, **golden**, and **rose**, with these variations:

- Almond: extra light almond, very light almond, light almond, light medium almond, medium almond, medium deep almond, deep almond, very deep almond, extra deep almond, and deepest almond
- Rose: very light rose, light rose, light medium rose, medium deep rose, deep rose, very deep rose, and extra deep rose

- Golden: very light golden, light golden, light medium golden, medium golden, medium deep golden, deep golden, and extra deep golden

You can even find YouTube tutorials on how to color realistic skin color with Crayola's "Colors of the World" colored pencils (Pamela's Passion for Pencils, 2021).

Laurel Greenfield's (2020) YouTube video on skin tones includes these recipes for creating warm skin tones.

For warm skin tones:

- Start with magenta, orange, medium yellow, or light yellow.
- Add a neutralizer, like a deep purple (dioxazine purple).
- Have white handy to lighten and desaturate.
- Adjust the color by adding various colors from the starting palette.

For a lighter pale pink/coral skin tone:

- Start with medium yellow.
- Add a little orange.
- Add some magenta.
- Add some white (lighten and desaturate).
- Adjust as needed:
  - If too yellow, add a little magenta.
  - If too orange, add a little yellow.
  - If too cold, add magenta for warmth.

For a middle brown skin tone:

- Start with a medium yellow.
- Add some orange.
- Add a little magenta to get a saturated orange.
- Add a tiny bit of purple to neutralize, for a deeper, richer brown.
- Adjust as needed.
  - To lighten, add a little medium yellow.
  - To lighten and desaturate, add a little white.
  - If too yellow, add a little magenta.

For a dark skin tone:

- Start with darker colors, like orange and purple, to get a rich, dark brown.
- Adjust as needed.
    - To lighten, add a bit of orange or medium yellow.
    - To darken, add purple.
    - For warmth, add orange.
    - For rosiness, add magenta.

These color combinations emphasize the wonderful diversity of skin tones.

With the basics of the traditional color wheel covered, let's look at how these colors relate to each other.

Chapter 6

Traditional RYB Primaries | Relationships on the Color Wheel

In addition to color mixing, the color wheel was created to help people choose colors that work well together. These 'formulas' provide a framework for the relationships between colors, known as color harmonies (SarahRenaeClark.com, 2023).

Color Formulas for Harmonious Color Schemes

The first image shows the color relationships on the Color Wheel.

© The Color Wheel Company™

Used with permission by The Color Wheel Company, PO Box 130, Philomath, OR 97370.

The second image shows a simple RYB color wheel that will be used to visually represent each color formula.

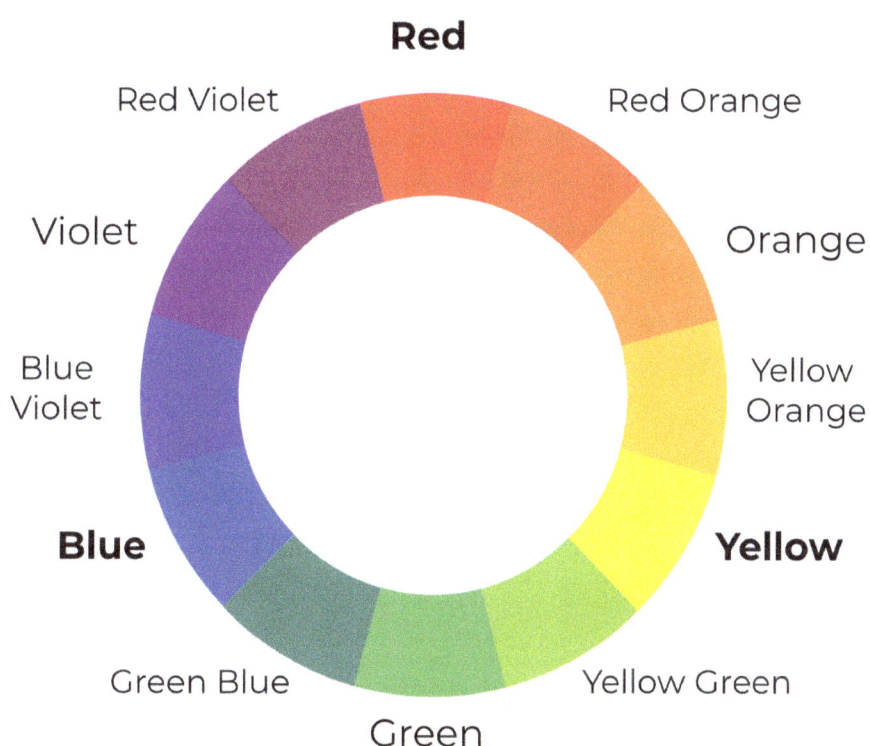

For each color formula, you will see a definition, color combinations representing the formula, and a visual. The definitions are from the *Color Wheel*™ (The Color Wheel Company) and *ColorSense* (Levin, 2008).

Achromatic is a "colorless" schema using blacks, whites, and grays. Think black-and-white photo.

- Colorless = no hue

RYB monochromatic color combinations use any shade, tint, or tone of just **one** color. This color palette is easy on the eyes, but it isn't the best choice for showing contrast. For example, you could use shades, tints, and tones of green.

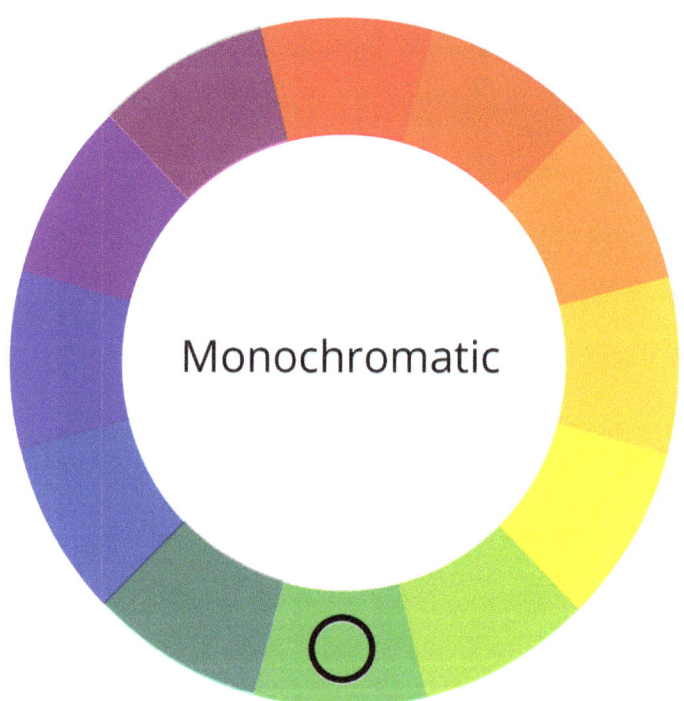

RYB analogous colors are hues next to each other on the color wheel. An analogous color scheme includes at least two but no more than five consecutive colors. They can include any shades, tints, or tones of those hues. Because they are side by side, there is little contrast. The colors 'match.' Examples:

- Green-blue, green, yellow-green
- Yellow, yellow-green, green, green-blue
- Blue, blue-violet, violet, red-violet, red

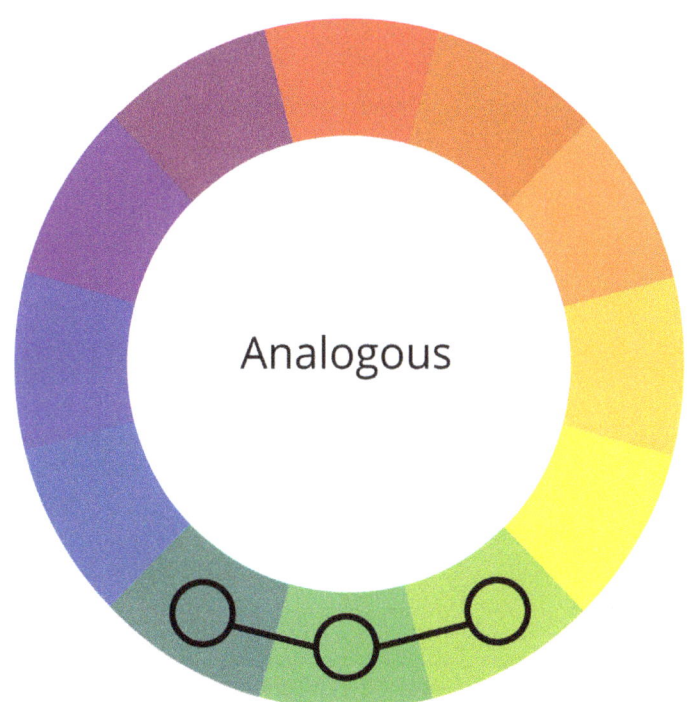

RYB complementary colors sit directly across from each other on the color wheel. They can include a shade, tint, or tone of one color, paired with the opposite color. Complementary colors intensify each other when placed together. They can be used to create high contrast and make shapes pop. Examples:

- Red and green
- Yellow and violet
- Blue and orange

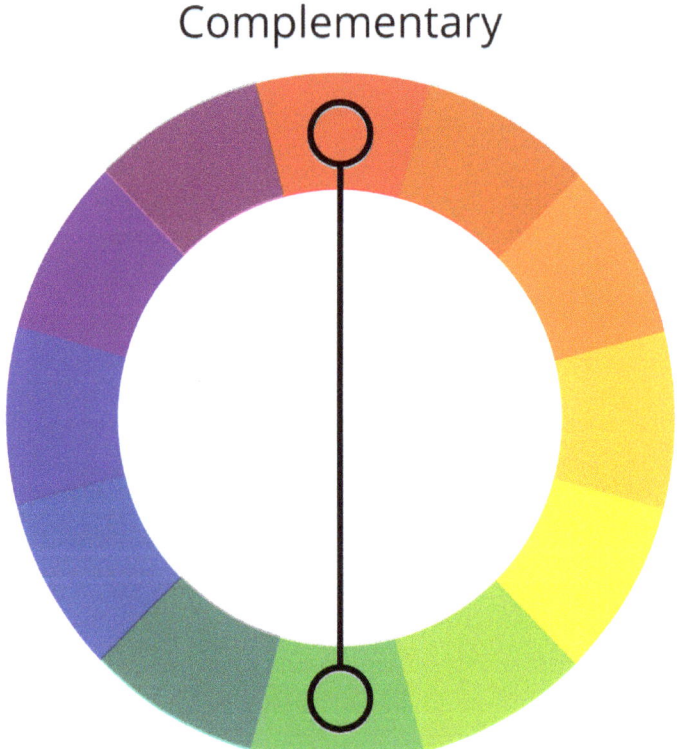

RYB split-complementary is one color plus the two colors on each side of the starting color's complement. This color palette is less intense than complementary colors. Examples:

- Green with red-orange and red-violet
- Blue with yellow-orange and red-orange
- Red with green-blue and yellow-green

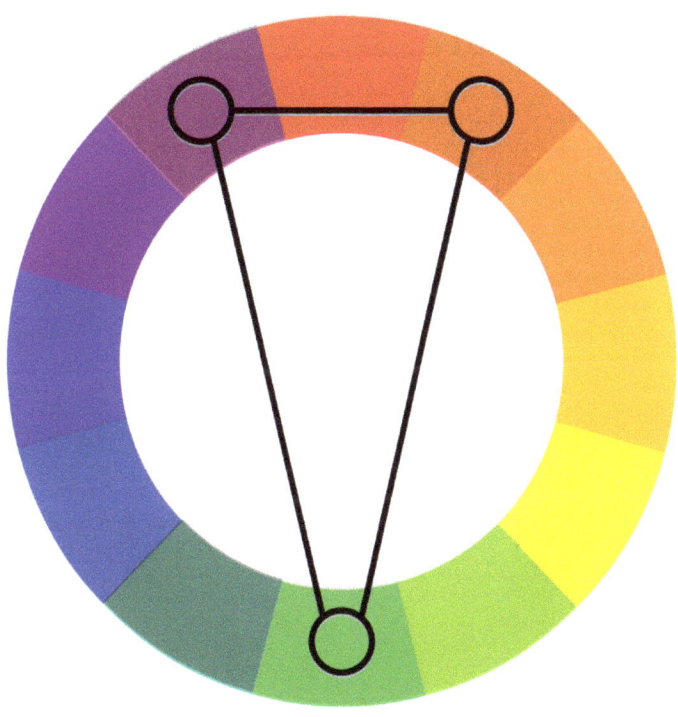

An **RYB triad (three-color combination)** is a color scheme with three colors equally spaced from each other on the color wheel. When used effectively, this palette feels like three best friends working well together (Malik, n.d.). Examples:

- Orange and violet and green
- Yellow and red and blue
- Red-violet and yellow-orange and blue-green
- Blue-violet and red-orange and yellow-green

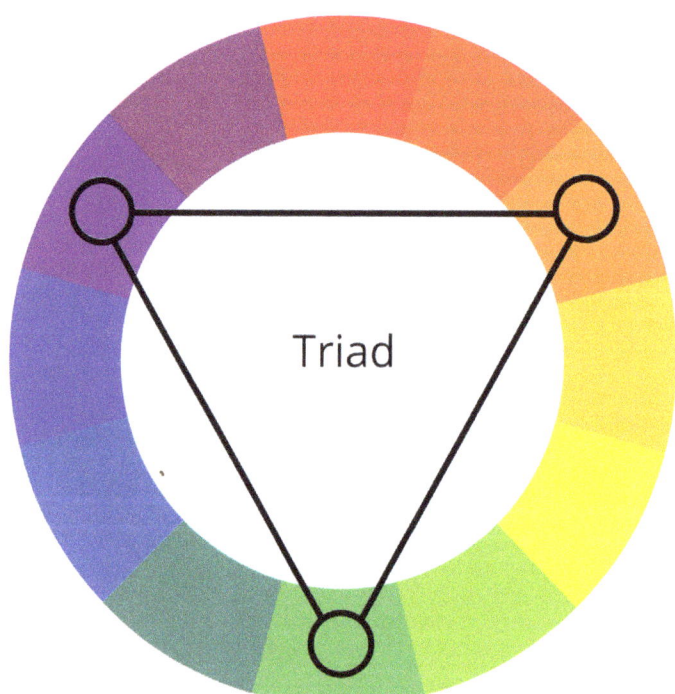

An **RYB tetrad (four-color combination)** uses two pairs of complementary colors for contrast. With tetrads, it is important to be intentional about how much of each color you use. Choose one color, possibly two, as the dominant color, with the others as accent colors. This helps avoid a cluttered and chaotic end product. Examples:

- Green and red with orange and blue
- Green and red with yellow-orange and blue-violet

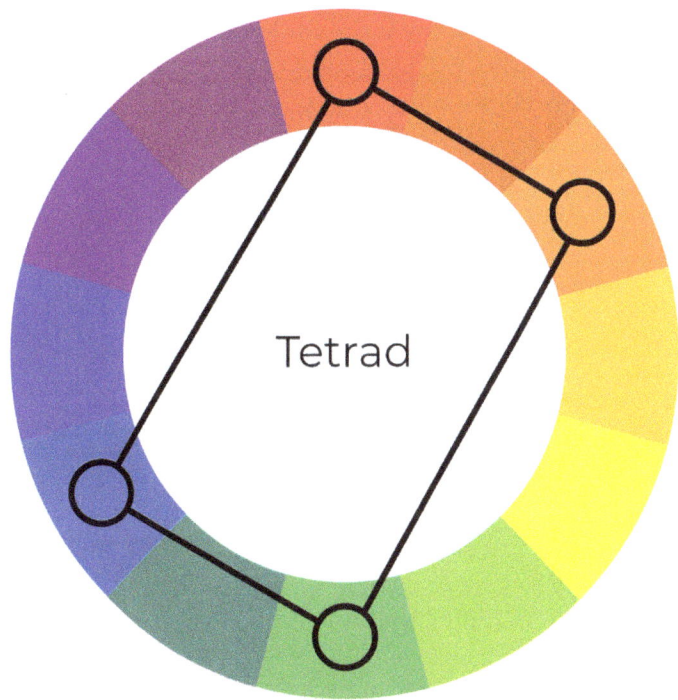

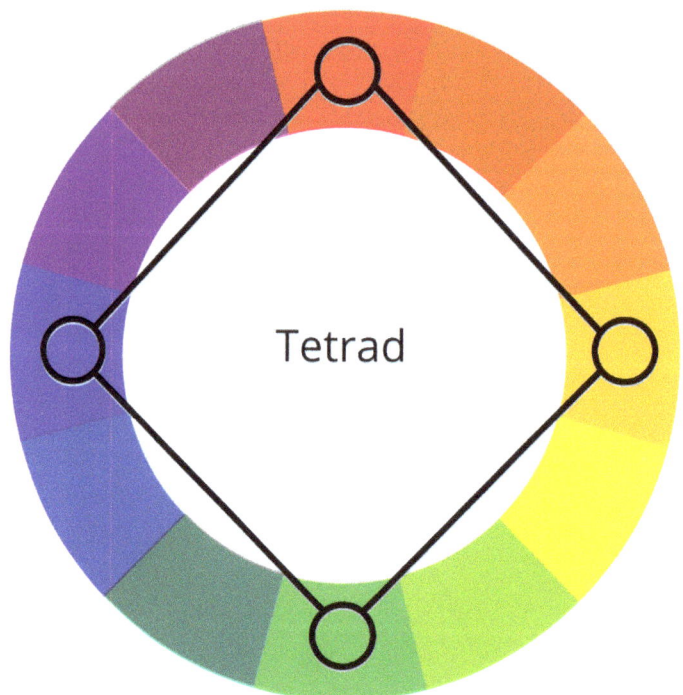

Using Color Formulas

Some creatives like to use the formulas to guide their experimentations, while others prefer to let the colors 'speak' to them, as if knowing what goes well together is in their DNA.

If you're relatively new to mixing and matching color, you may find it helpful to use a formula to create harmony.

Here's how to get started with color formulas:

1. Select a formula: monochromatic, analogous, complementary, split-complementary, triad, or tetrad.
2. Pick one dominant color.
3. Follow the formula to add colors.

Tip: Look for color schemes in the world around you. To find the color combinations you're drawn to, create a mood board of colorful items that evoke an emotional response—such as photos, color palettes from the paint store, or swatches of cloth. This exercise will help you start to identify colors related to your authentic self.

Now let's move from traditional primaries to modern primaries.

Chapter 7

Modern CMY Primaries on the Color Wheel

Modern primaries are the 'other' type of subtractive **primary colors** made from **reflected** light. These two color scales, however, require us to flip the very definition of what a primary color is. What?!

- **Traditional primaries** are colors that **cannot** be mixed from any other colors.
    - RYB (red, yellow, and blue)
- **Modern primaries** are colors from which (nearly) all other colors can be obtained **by mixing**. Seriously? Yes...
    - CMY (cyan, magenta, and yellow)

Mind-blowing.

Artists, designers, artisans, students, and amateurs can start with these modern primaries (cyan, magenta, and yellow) to create colors, such as vibrant green, that aren't possible when starting with red, yellow, and blue. (Wow!)

Modern Primaries (CMY) use a combination of these colors:

- **C**yan (a turquoise blue)
- **M**agenta
- **Y**ellow

Sometimes you will see CMYK instead of CMY:

- **C**yan (a turquoise blue)
- **M**agenta
- **Y**ellow
- Blac**K**

I was familiar with CMYK because I've had to replace printer cartridges. Now I understand the application of this color model extends beyond the world of print. It's quite amazing!

Originally, the "K" stood for the key color used on the key plate for printing, which was typically black. Now the "K" simply stands for BlacK. When you see CMY or CMYK, they are essentially referring to the same thing.

These triads (cyan, magenta, yellow) are combined to form nearly all visible colors. When modern primaries are combined in equal amounts, the result is black—no color is reflected.[7]

---

[7] © "RGB Color Samples" by Canva creator Oleska 2024

Note the CMY colors in the images above:

- Primary colors: cyan, magenta, yellow
- Secondary colors: red, blue, green
- All colors (overlapping in the center): black

CMY Color Wheel (Front)

The *CMY Primary Mixing Wheel*™ is another color mixing tool used to show the "subtractive color spectrum, tints, tones, shades, and color relationships" (colorwheelco.com). This color wheel serves a similar purpose to the traditional color wheel. The key difference lies in the starting hues of cyan, magenta, and yellow.

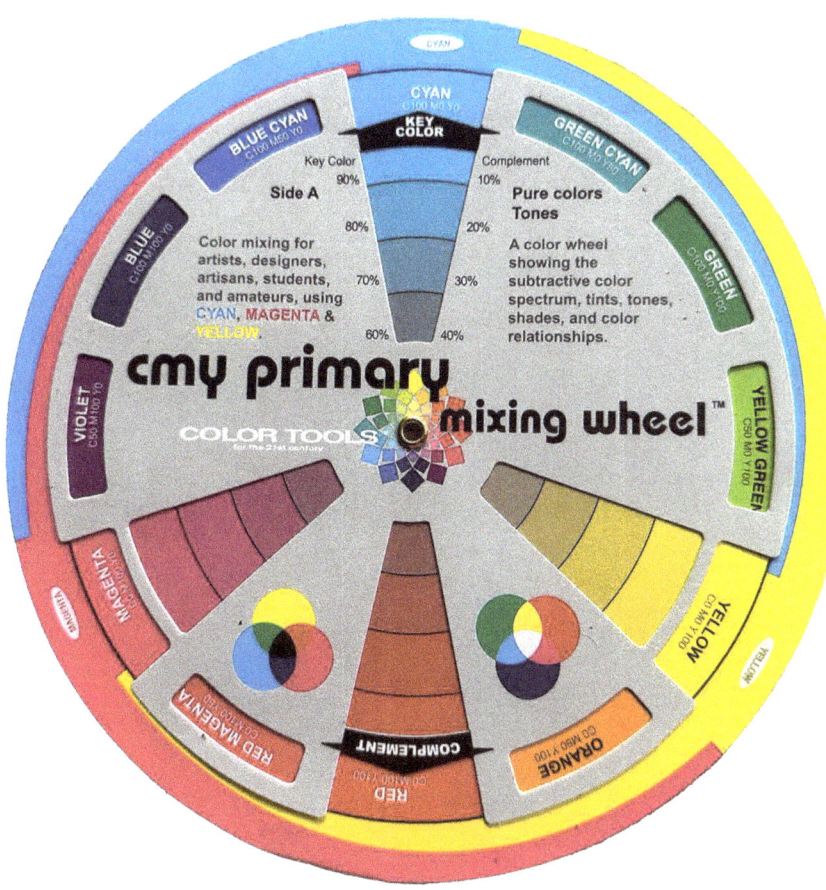

CMY Color Wheel (Back)

© The Color Wheel Company™ 2024

Used with permission by The Color Wheel Company, PO Box 130, Philomath, OR 97370.

CMY Color Definitions

The following definitions are from the CMY Primary Mixing Wheel (above).

Primary colors:

- Colors from which nearly all other colors can be obtained by mixing
- Cyan, magenta, yellow (CMY)

Secondary colors:

- Each secondary color is made by mixing two primary colors:
    - Cyan + Magenta = Blue
    - Cyan + Yellow = Green
    - Yellow + Magenta = Red

Tertiary colors:

- Six colors, each made by mixing one primary with an adjacent secondary color:
    - Yellow + Red = **Orange**
    - Yellow + Green = **Yellow-green (e.g., chartreuse)**
    - Green + Cyan = **Green-cyan (e.g., spring green)**
    - Blue + Cyan = **Blue cyan (e.g., azure)**
    - Magenta + Blue = **Violet**
    - Red + Magenta = **Red-magenta (e.g., rose)**

Color Variations

In the context of Modern Primaries, **hues** are the twelve colors in the outer ring of the CMY Primary Mixing Wheel: orange, red, red-magenta, magenta, violet, blue, blue-cyan, cyan, cyan-green, green, yellow-green, and yellow.

The **values** (i.e., the relative lightness or darkness of a color) are shown on Side B of the CMY Primary Mixing Wheel for 20/40/60/80 percent tints and 20/40/60/80 percent shades:

- Shades: Color + black to deepen the value
- Tints: Color + white to lighten the value
- Tones: [Color + gray] or [color + the color's complement]

Referring to the CMY Primary Mixing Wheel is particularly helpful if you're not familiar with CMYK, which is often the case because this color model is not typically taught in school.

> So, which color wheel is the best? Artist's Primaries (RYB) or Printer's Primaries (CMYK)?
>
> This is a highly debated and controversial topic among artists, scientists, philosophers, and mathematicians. **This was news to me. Anyone else?**
>
> Check out Sarah Renae Clark's YouTube video on "Controversial Color Theory" for a fabulous explanation of:
>
> - the history of the color wheels
> - an updated definition of 'primary color'
> - pros and cons of each color wheel
>
> Key takeaway: Pick one set of primaries—RYB or CMY—as a starting point to guide you on your color experimentation journey.

CMYK System for Printers

The CMYK color scale is commonly used for color printing and reproduction because of its wide gamut of color combinations and vibrancy.

Common printers use different proportions of cyan, magenta, yellow, and black to create a variety of print-friendly colors for use with white paper. Colored words and images are created when tiny dots (halftones) of varying sizes and amounts of CMYK ink are printed.

Try using the CMYK Calculator[8] to see how changing the percent for each color impacts the color to be printed.

---

[8] *W3 Schools is a web developer site for learning how to code:* https://www.w3schools.com/colors/colors_cmyk.asp

0 percent of each = white

0 percent of each except for 100 percent of Cyan = Cyan (cyan ink reflects cyan wavelength).

0 percent of each except for 100 percent magenta = magenta (magenta ink reflects magenta wavelength).

CMYK Calculator

0 percent of each except for 100 percent yellow = yellow (yellow ink reflects yellow wavelength).

CMYK Calculator

0 percent of each except for 100 percent black = black (black ink absorbs nearly all wavelengths and reflects none).

Other ways to print black (not shown):

- 100 percent of each except for 0 percent black = black (or near black) = (black ink absorbs nearly all wavelengths).
- 100 percent of each (C/M/Y/K) = black.

CMYK Calculator

```
cmyk(0%, 0%, 0%, 100%)
rgb(0, 0, 0)
#000000
hsl(0, 0%, 0%)
```

C: 0 [0]
M: 0 [0]
Y: 0 [0]
K: 100 [100]

LIVING AUTHENTICALLY THROUGH COLOR

50 percent cyan, 0 percent magenta, 50 percent yellow, 0 percent black = a shade of green (the green ink reflects the green wavelengths).

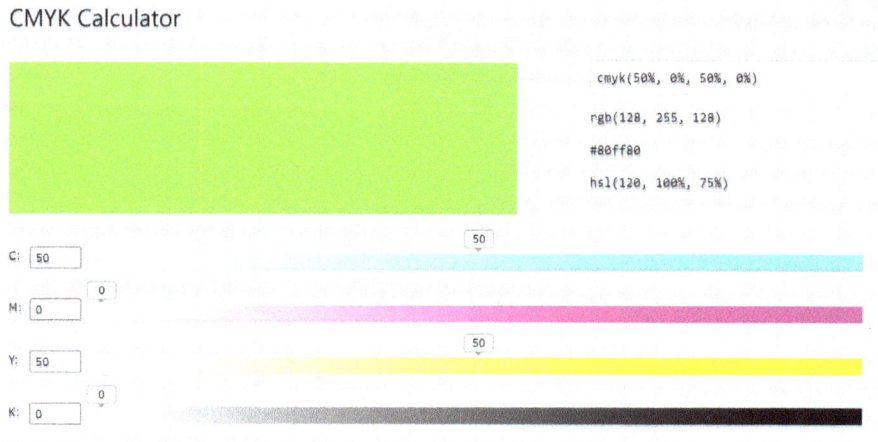

CMYK colors are known for printing vivid colors consistently and are often used for product labeling, photos, and magazines. The key to consistency, however, is accurate color calibration of the printing equipment, which isn't always reliable.

CMYK Is Subtractive

Circling back, what makes CMY/CMYK primaries subtractive? Refresh my memory, please.

CMYK is **subtractive** because the absorbed light waves are **subtracted** (filtered) from what is visible (reflected).

- Stating the obvious, the absence of ink on white paper produces white color.
  - White absorbs no color; white reflects all colors equally.
- If you print 100 percent cyan ink and no other MYK inks, the cyan reduces the brightness of the white and reflects cyan light wavelengths.
- Adding black will always darken your printing. If you want vibrant colors, best avoid adding black.
- The presence of all CMYK inks produces a black color.

- Black absorbs all the light equally; black reflects none.
- For a pure looking black, the key component of black ink is important.
  - CMY = a dark color that looks like black.
  - CMYK = a much darker, purer looking black.

Note: More printing tips to come after addressing RBG, the mixing of light. (●●●)

Now let's look at color relationships for modern primaries. The formulas are the same as those shared for traditional primaries, but the starting colors are different.

Chapter 8

Modern CMY Primaries | Relationships on the Color Wheel

The color formula definitions for traditional primaries also apply to modern primaries—but the actual colors vary by color model.

Color Formulas for Harmonious Color Schemes

This image shows a simple CMY color wheel that will be used to visually represent each color formula.

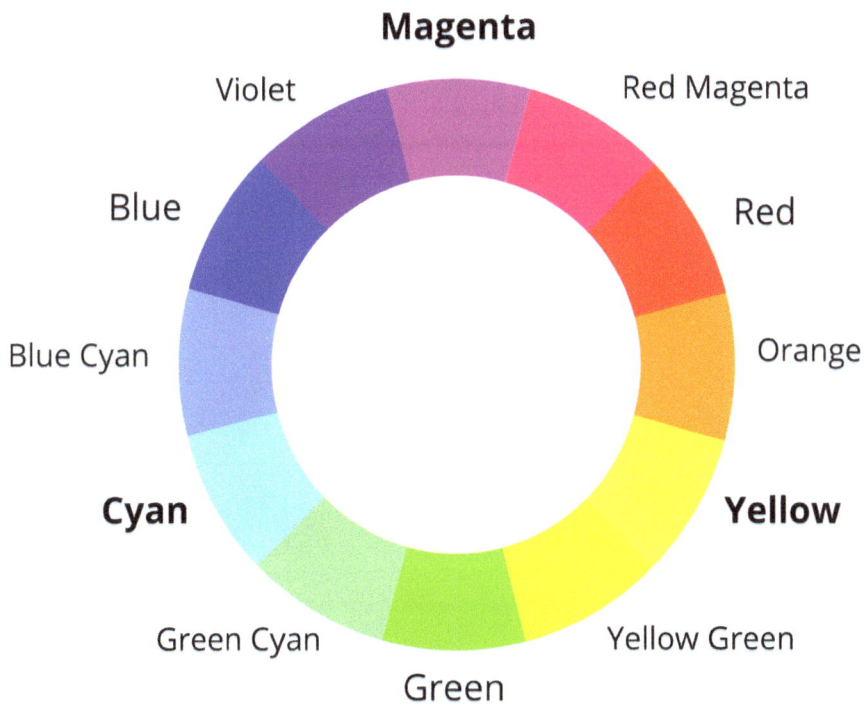

For each color formula, you will see a definition, color combinations representing the formula, and a visual. The definitions are from the *Color Wheel* (The Color Wheel Company) and *ColorSense* (Levin, 2008).

CMY analogous colors are hues next to each other on the color wheel. An analogous color scheme includes at least two, but no more than five, consecutive colors. These schemes can include any shades, tints, or tones of those hues. Because they are side-by-side, there is little contrast. These colors "match."

Examples of analogous colors using CMY primaries:

- Yellow-green, green, green-cyan
- Cyan, green-cyan
- Orange, red, red-magenta
- Violet, blue, blue-cyan, cyan

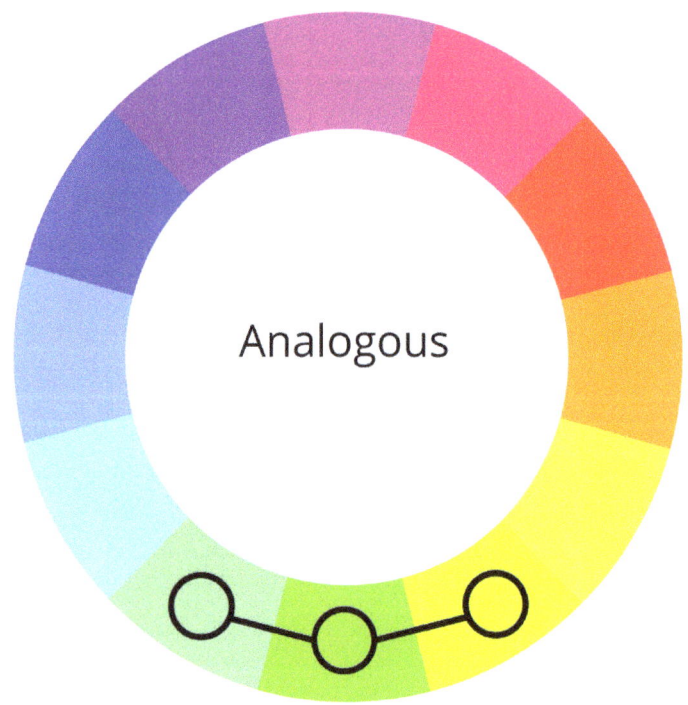

CMY complementary colors, also known as complementary hues, are directly across from each other on the color wheel. This scheme can include a shade, tint, or tone of one color and the opposite color. Complementary colors intensify each other when placed together. Examples:

- Magenta and green
- Cyan and red
- Yellow-green and violet
- Yellow and blue
- Orange and blue-cyan
- Red-magenta and green-cyan

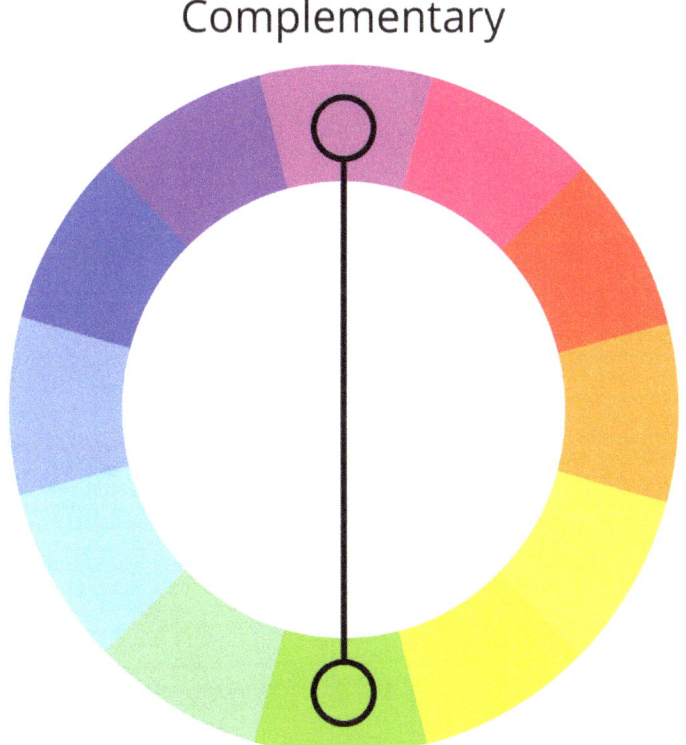

CMY split-complementary colors consist of one color plus the two colors adjacent to its complement on the color wheel.

Examples:

- If green is the starting color, then the split-complementary colors are green, violet, and red-magenta because:
    - Magenta is green's complement.
    - Violet and red-magenta are on either side of magenta.
- If cyan is the starting color, then the split-complementary colors are cyan, orange, and red-magenta because:
    - Red is cyan's complement.
    - Orange and red-magenta are on either side of red.
- Red, blue-cyan, and green-cyan
- Blue, yellow-green, and orange
- Violet, green, and yellow

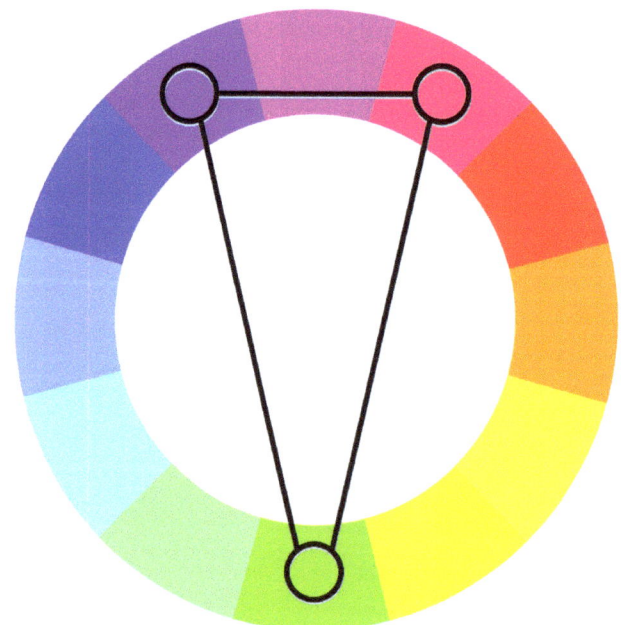

A **CMY triad (three-color combination)** is a color scheme using three colors equally spaced from each other on the color wheel. Examples:

- Red, green, and blue
- Red-magenta, yellow-green, and blue-cyan
- Magenta, yellow, and cyan
- Violet, orange, and green-cyan

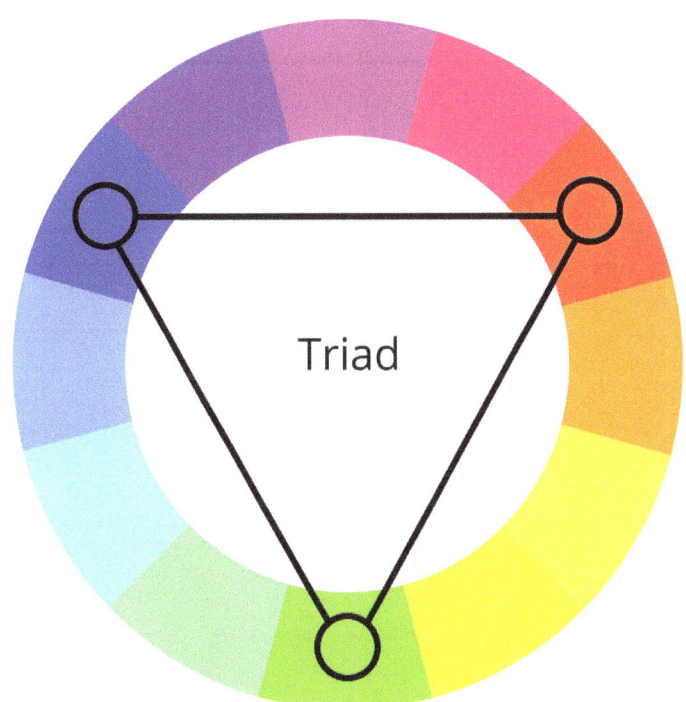

A **CMY tetrad (four-color combination)** uses two pairs of complements for contrast. Examples:

- Magenta and green with red and cyan
- Magenta and green with orange and blue-cyan

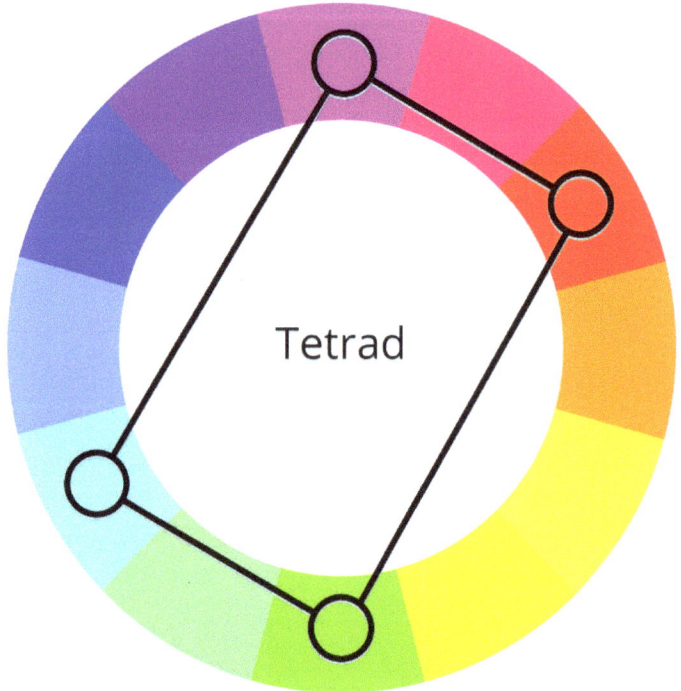

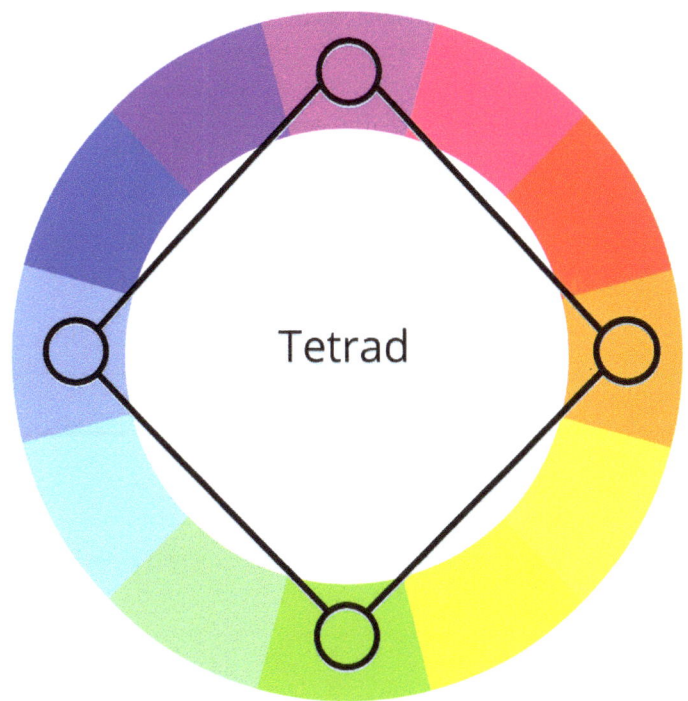

I was blown away by the CMY Primary Color Wheel. Anyone else?

Visual Communication

There is more to the story than color relationships. While it's helpful to understand why and when to use monochromatic instead of complementary, or triad instead of analogous, other design elements can elevate the end product. When creating something visual—a painting, quilt, garden, graphic, or waiting room—**color** is a critical element in **setting the mood**. If you want to learn more, check out videos by Gareth David on YouTube (2016) as a starting point. His videos include information about these graphic design principles: contrast, hierarchy, alignment, balance, proximity, repetition, simplicity, and function.

Up Next: Travel back in time to 1666 and the discovery of my inspirational friend, Roy G. Biv, whose fame relates to the mixing of light and the colors of the rainbow. Surprisingly enough, RGB is the color model of mixing light, but RGB does not stand for Roy G. Biv. (●●●)

Chapter 9

RGB Additive Primary Colors | The Mixing of Light

In 1666, Sir Isaac Newton, at age twenty-three, used science to keep busy during the lockdown of the Great Plague of London. He experimented with prisms, mirrors, and light, resulting in several revolutionary discoveries. His breakthrough findings are the basis for many of our first science lessons on color and light.

Among Newton's discoveries:

- Sunlight is made of a seemingly infinite number of colors. He chose to limit the list to seven core colors to align with seven notes on the music scale. Hence, the birth of Roy G Biv, which stands for **R**ed, **O**range, **Y**ellow, **G**reen, **B**lue, **I**ndigo, and **V**iolet.
- Color is part of the electromagnetic spectrum that we can see, aka the 'visible' spectrum.

- - Humans cannot see other parts of the electromagnetic spectrum: radio waves, microwaves, infrared, ultraviolet, x-rays, and gamma rays.
  - Each color is a unique wavelength with a frequency, measured in nanometers (nm), identifying how quickly the wave travels.
    - The human eye can detect wavelengths within a range of 380-700 nm.
    - Red is the longest wavelength (lowest frequency).
    - Violet is the shortest wavelength (highest frequency).

Light Waves of Color: Primary and Secondary Colors

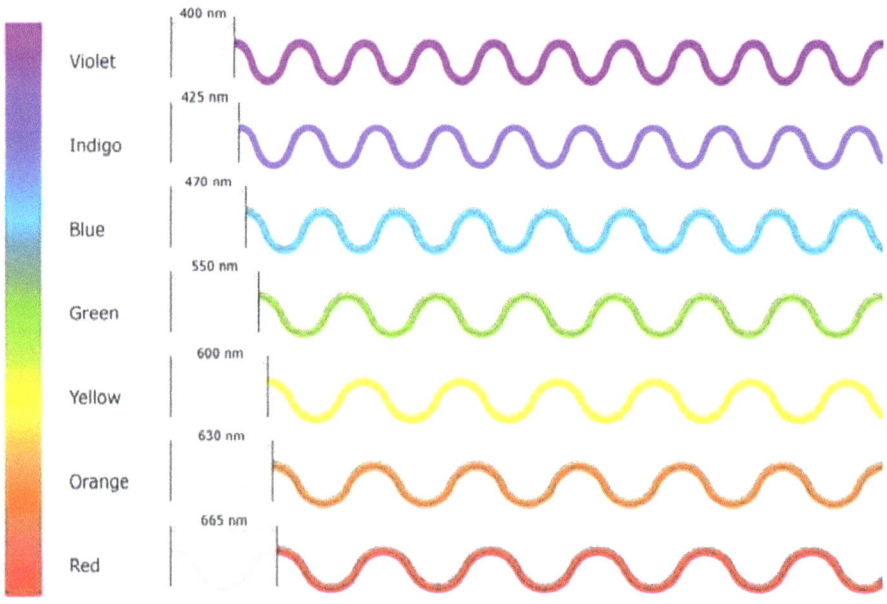

Used with permission. © The University of Waikato Te Whare Wānanga o Waikato | www.sciencelearn.org.nz

When mixed, these wavelength combinations form distinct colors based on the frequencies of the light waves being reflected.

Equal parts red light, green light, and blue light (R+G+B) create clear white light. That's why, according to Newton, when "mixing" light waves, the primary colors are red, green, and blue (RGB). Wait. What?! (●●●)

Another way to say it:

Additive primary colors—red, green, and blue (RGB)—are made from light waves. As you blend **(add)** different combinations of RGB light waves, you get new colors.

If you shine three flashlights, so the spotlight overlaps, the light is brighter compared to one or two flashlights. Right? That's because **adding** light **adds** brightness.

If you **add** a transparent colored filter to each flashlight—one red, one green, and one blue—you get a bright new color. The image below shows what happens when you overlap the three beams of **red, green,** and **blue** light.[9]

---

[9] © "RGB Color Model Logo" by Canva creator Oleska 2024

What you see:
- Blue light + Green light = Cyan (turquoise blue) light
- Red light + Blue light = Magenta (dark pink) light
- Red light + Green light = Yellow light
  - For real?! Yep. Mixing colored light is **not** the same as mixing pigments and dyes.
- Red light + Blue light + Green light = White light
  - Remember, white light absorbs no color. Instead, white reflects all colors equally.

RGB are primary colors of light because all colors can be made from them *(not because eye receptors respond optimally to red, green, and blue.)*

RGB may sound familiar to you because this is how your computer and TV screens work. (●●●)

Cyan, magenta, and yellow are secondary colors of light because they are the result of adding two primary colors of light.

The following color pairs are **complementary colors** because they 'complete' each other when mixed. Notice how they are directly across from each other in the Venn diagram.

- Blue light + Yellow light = White light
- Red light + Cyan light = White light
- Green light + Magenta light = White light

Fun fact: Modern CMY primaries and RGB light primaries—are opposites of each other. The primary colors of one are secondary colors of the other (Sarah Renae Clark, 2023). See Appendix A for images.

Colors on a Screen

Colors you see digitally on screens—like computer monitors, TVs, cameras, mobile phones, and color scanners—are based on wavelengths of light.

All the colors you see on a screen are combinations of red, green, and blue (RGB) light wavelengths. The quality of the screen and the intensity of the light source inside the device influence the number and quality of colors. (Think high-definition TVs.)

There are 256 wavelength options for red, 256 for green, and 256 for blue, ranging from 0–255 each. This translates to 16,777,216 combinations, or colors. Wow!

For example, this wavelength combination is this orange:

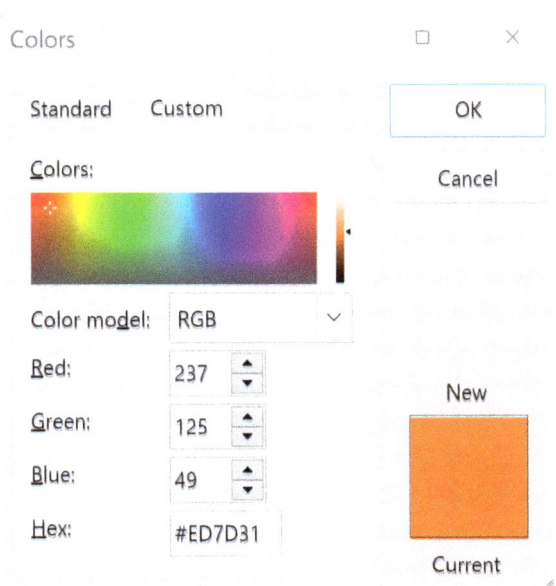

LIVING AUTHENTICALLY THROUGH COLOR   63

It takes three digits to identify the value for each red, green, and blue wavelength, for a total of nine digits: 237, 125, 049.

These nine digits can be translated into a six-digit HEX code, which is a hexadecimal way to express the RGB code in six characters (numbers, letters, or a combination of the two). Not only is HEX code shorter and easier to type, but it also works well with binary computer code.

If you choose "custom" when formatting color in Microsoft Word, for example, you can play around to see how adding and subtracting individually from either red, green, or blue (0–255) changes the product. In the images below, notice the HEX code and how it changes, too.

As you **add** different combinations of RGB light waves, you get new colors. Again, this is why RGB colors are called **additive.**

Examples:

Mixing at the lowest degree is black: RGB (0, 0, 0) | HEX (#000000)

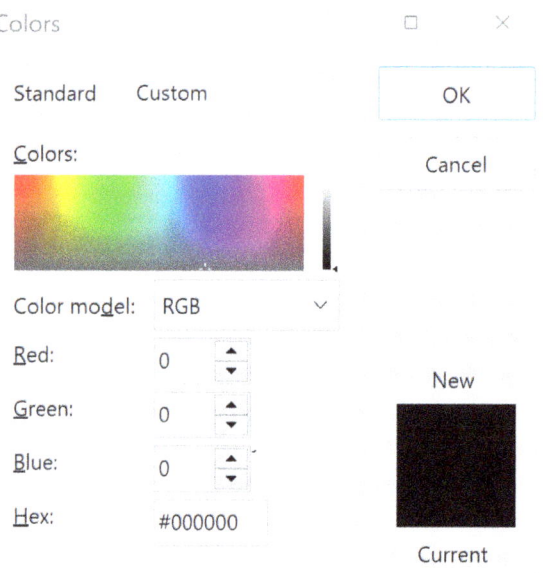

Mixing at the highest degree is pure white: RGB (255, 255, 255) | HEX (#FFFFFF)

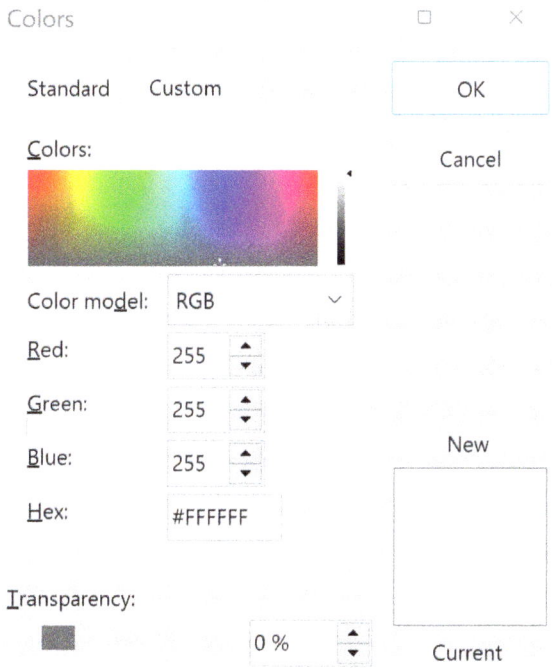

If you were to change the combinations, you would discover these HEX codes:

Pure red = RGB (255, 0, 0) | HEX (#FF0000)
Pure green = RGB (0, 255, 0) | HEX (#00FF00)
Pure blue = RGB (0, 0, 255) | HEX (#0000FF)

This pink: RGB (255, 102, 255) | HEX (#FF66FF)

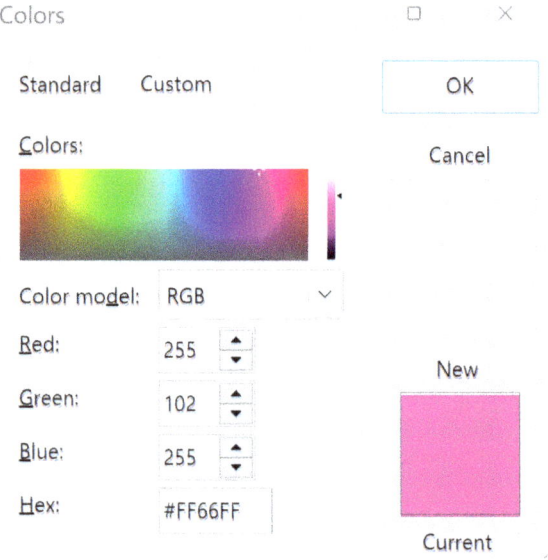

FFFFFF Hex Codes

But why "FFFFFF"?

HEX code uses a hexadecimal number system, so "255" can be written as two digits instead of three. Again, this is helpful for coding purposes.

Here's what the conversion looks like if you want to know the 'why.'

HEX code writes 1–9 as two digits:
00, 01, 02, 03, 04, 05, 06, 07, 08, 09

And then introduces six letters to represent 10–15 (i.e., A–F):
10=A, 11=B, 12=C, 13=D, 14=E, 15=F

Then, standard counting (10–19) picks up from where the 0–9 left off.
16=10, 17=11, 18=12, 19=13, 20=14, 21=15, 22=16, 23=17, 24=18, 25=19

Like the counting changed at "09," it also shifts at 19 and is written as "1" + (letters A – F):
26=1A, 27=1B, 28=1C, 29=1D, 30=1E, 31=1F

This pattern continues and repeats until 255. *See Appendix B for a full translation.*

Examples of colors and their RGB and HEX codes:

Vivid Orange		
RGB	Value	Conversion to HEX
Red	255	FF
Green	153	99
Blue	000	00
		#FF9900

Cornflower Blue		
RGB	Value	Conversion to HEX
Red	102	66
Green	153	99
Blue	255	FF
		#6699FF

Light Gray		
RGB	Value	Conversion to HEX
Red	210	D2
Green	210	D2
Blue	210	D2
		#D2D2D2

RGB and HEX codes identify how much red, green, and blue are in a digital color. While the RGB model is relatively straightforward, it doesn't allow for making colors lighter or darker or paler or richer.

Adjusting Colors Digitally

There are other tools available for adjusting how digital colors display. For example, in Adobe Photoshop, you can change the gradient, brightness and contrast, vibrance, hue and saturation, highlights and shadows, and so on.

Depending on the software, you may have seen these acronyms:

- HSB = Hue, Saturation, Brightness
- HSV = Hue, Saturation, Value
- HSL = Hue, Saturation, Lightness

HSB and HSV Color Models

The HSB and HSV color models allow you to describe colors (hue or tint) in terms of their shade (saturation or amount of gray) and their brightness (value or luminance) of an RGB color (Tursucular, n.d.). These color models also enable you to adjust an RGB color.

Hue (H) is the pure color on a scale of 0°–360° based on its degree on the color wheel.[10]

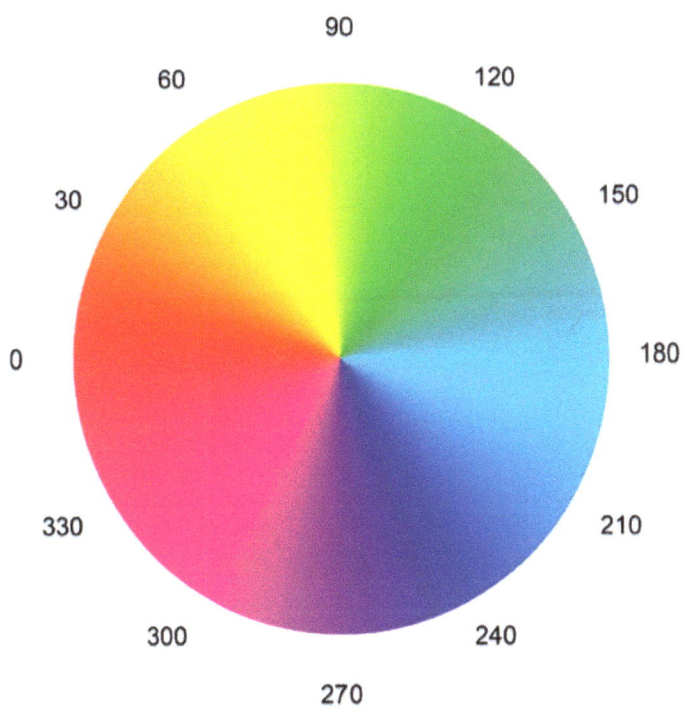

- 0 red
- 30 orange
- 60 yellow
- 90 yellow-green
- 120 green
- 150 green-blue
- 180 cyan
- 210 blue-green
- 240 blue
- 270 violet
- 300 magenta
- 330 blue-red / red-violet

---

[10] © "Color wheel spectrum" by Canva creator GlitterKlo 2024

Saturation (S) is how rich the color is on a scale of 0–100 percent.

- 100 percent is the richest variant
- 0 percent is the palest variant (always a grayish color)

Lighting causes saturation to increase or decrease. Have you ever noticed how the color of a room changes based on the time of day and lighting?

- Color is more vivid when exposed to daylight because it's highly saturated.
- Color is duller at twilight because it's desaturated.

Brightness (B) or **Value (V)** is how bright the color is on a scale of 0–100 percent. Brightness relates to the amount of white added to a hue; the more white, the greater the vibrance.

- 100 percent is the brightest color
- 0 percent is the darkest color (always black)

Adjusting vibrance only affects dull or cool tones and can bring them to life. This is particularly helpful in photography because adjustments don't impact skin tones.

Regardless of Hue:

- If Saturation = 0% and Brightness = 100%, the result is always White.
- If Saturation = 100% and Brightness = 0%, the result is always Black. Why? No light = no color.

HSL Model

The HSL model (Hue, Saturation, Lightness) is not the same as HSV and HSB. HSL is used to easily adjust colors in digital formats, such as photography, graphics, videos, and web design.

For example, HSL tuning sliders are used to edit photos and videos.

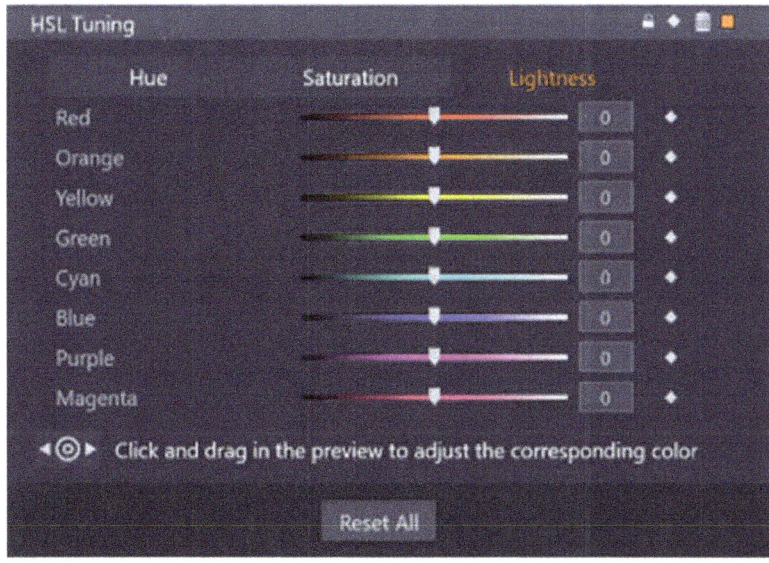

Additionally, HSL is used in web design because it simplifies the process of changing colors in HTML (HyperText Markup Language) code and CSS (Cascading Style Sheets). Instead of using a six-digit code like the HEX code, which requires interpretation, the HSL code is easily readable and adjustable.

For example, **HSL (300, 100%, 50%)** is a bright magenta: 300 is magenta hue, 100% is full saturation, and 50% lightness. This change in HSL would change the background from bright magenta to a teal color in one easy step.

```
<style>
div {
    background-color: hsl (170, 50%, 50%);
    color: hsl ( 0%, 50%, 50%);
}
</style>
```

Color Pickers

Color pickers are tools in various software products that allow users to select and adjust a color's hue, saturation, and brightness/value/lightness. Color picker tools can include interactive components, manual entry, or an eyedropper to select a color from an existing image.

To play around with different representations of HEX and RGB colors, search your browser for "HEX to RGB" or try these websites with various interactive widgets:

- **Rapid Tables**[11]
    - Check out the RGB Color Picker, RGB Color Codes Chart, RGB color space, etc.

---

[11] https://www.rapidtables.com/web/color/RGB_Color.html

- **W3Schools**[12] is for web developers
    - Enter or pick a color in the HTML Color Picker. Then look at the color swatches and HSL information in the tables for Hue, Saturation, and Lightness.
- **Adobe Color**[13] is a wonderful site to practice some of the concepts about color.
    - Click the "Help (?)" icon in the top menu for a quick start guide.
    - Click "Accessibility Tools" to check color contrast, an important step to ensure text is legible.
- **Colour Contrast Checker**[14] is an easy, go-to option for checking accessibility
- **Who Can Use**[15] shows how color contrast can affect people with visual impairments.

Reminder: While RGB provides numerous colors in digital format, the color matching system between digital and printing, for example, can limit or expand printing capabilities of those RGB colors.

---

[12] https://www.w3schools.com/colors/colors_picker.asp
[13] https://color.adobe.com/create/color-wheel
[14] https://colourcontrast.cc/
[15] https://www.whocanuse.com/

Chapter 10

The Best Color Model for Printing

It is important to plan ahead if you're printing something you want to look professional. This chapter summarizes common file types, their pros and cons for printing, and color models in the context of printing.

File Formats for Printing

A digital file is required to print. A person can print a Microsoft Word document (.docx) in color, for example, but what file types are used for printing graphics, images, and drawings?

Here are common file formats (Ellis, 2022):

- **Portable Document Format (PDF)** is a common format for sharing files for things like program guides or booklets; however, the images aren't scalable.
- **Joint Photographic Experts Group (JPEG/JPG)** is used for images. JPEGs use less data (than PNGs) because they always

have a white background. JPEGs are rastor (not vector), meaning they are pixel-based. These images get pixelated (grainy) when enlarged.
- **Portable Network Graphics (PNG)** is another format for images. PNGs have a clear background, which translates to a larger file size than JPG/JPEG. These images are also rastor (pixel-based).
- **Graphics Interchange Format (GIF)** is a format often used for logos or images with large areas of flat color; however, GIFs do not handle gradients well.
- **Scalable Vector Graphic (SVG)** is a good format for line drawings. SVG is vector (not rastor), meaning it's all lines. As in the name, SVG is scalable; it can scale down to the size of a penny and scale up to the size of a building. SVG is also sharp and clear.
- **Encapsulated PostScript (EPS)** is a vector-based format. It is not used for the web.
- **Adobe Illustrator (Ai)** files are vector-based. They have a transparent background and can hold RGB or CMYK really well. This format is scalable, too, meaning the graphics, drawings, and images can be enlarged with no impact on resolution.
- The **Adobe Photoshop (PSD)** format holds color really well. A PSD has an impressive range of height and width and can store multiple layers, images, and objects.

Color Theory Models (revisited)

RGB

If you are designing for digital consumption (i.e., for online use only), use RGB additive primaries. This includes graphics and video recordings used on websites, apps, and social media. Common RGB formats include JPG, PNG, GIF, and PSD.

CMYK Over RGB

Important note: If you plan to **print** something physically, especially something you will be selling, it is best to **design using modern CMY**

primaries, not additive primaries (RGB) for digital use. This is because there are many RGB colors that you cannot achieve in CMYK, such as bright blues, bright greens, or vibrant royal purple. If you design in RGB with the expectation of printing in CMYK with the same vibrancy, you may be disappointed.

CMYK or PMS?

Perhaps you have heard of the Pantone Matching System (PMS). Wait—another acronym?

Pantone prides itself on precision and accuracy across all formats—online, print, merchandise, etc. Because Pantone prints each color separately (instead of color mixing, as with CMYK primaries), color matching is consistent regardless of the printer. However, because multiple colors require multiple rounds of printing, this can translate to higher production costs—something larger companies justify for a consistent brand experience.

Pantone's wide range also accommodates vibrant colors, like bright blues and greens, as well as metallic or neon colors. If color choice and lower cost are more important than absolute precision, CMYK is sufficient. It ultimately comes down to weighing the pros and cons for your project.

If you want to see how colors convert from CMYK to PMS, and vice versa, check out the **CMYK to Pantone color converter.**[16]

An Amazing World of Printed Color

The printing choices we have in the twenty-first century are extraordinary. You can print amazingly bright colors on virtually any surface.

Check out the Confetti Dreamers Pinterest page[17] for some creative examples, such as:

---

[16] https://www.ginifab.com/feeds/pms/cmyk_to_pantone.php *Note: Ginifab is a mid-size graphic design company operating the e-commerce site ginifab.com and warn users to use their tool for reference only. Before printing, they recommend confirming the color match with real printed Pantone guides.*

[17] https://www.pinterest.com/ConfettiDreamers/

- plastic wraps on cars, utility boxes, and skyscrapers
- photo prints on canvas
- colored prints on PVC or metal sheets
- signage of any size
- laser engraving on wood
- stickers

The possibilities are nearly endless. With the basics of *three* color models (who would've thought!?) and color formulas for creating harmony, let's move on to color psychology principles. The principles of color psychology apply to all colors, regardless of the medium.

Chapter 11

Color Psychology

Color psychology is the study of how color influences emotional response, perception, and behavior. Research in this area is used by designers and marketers to persuade potential buyers to make purchases and increase brand loyalty. As much as we may not want to admit it, the bottom line of design and marketing is all about making money.

A Brand's Color Story

In a capitalist market where profit is a priority, a brand's color story can literally influence a consumer's purchase decision within the first ninety seconds (SRV Media, 2023). From the colors used on a candy bar wrapper to a fast-food logo, color is used to lure you in with the overall message being, "Buy me." However, it doesn't stop there. Color can also influence your choice of bank, the realty company you use, and other high-dollar purchase decisions. Color combination is a powerful tool, indeed.

Although our individual perception of color is unique based on genetics and personal experiences, brand experts use **color meanings, symbolism,** and **color theory** with great intention to elicit a positive customer response.

Brand experts interlace facets of color psychology with company purpose to create a cohesive image.

A company's brand includes:

- their story
- personality (guided by keywords and characteristics)
- purpose or cause
- target audience(s)
- messaging
- **color palette (color story)**

When choosing a color palette, brand experts look at competitors to find patterns, as well as differentiators. *They want to fit in, but they also want to stand out.* Selecting a color formula is a great place to start (see Chapters 6–8). As a reminder, a color palette usually has a primary focal color, along with accent colors.

It's also important for a brand's color palette to align with its personality. For example, bright colors are fun and modern, whereas desaturated colors (gray tones) are more business-like. When choosing colors to reflect a brand's personality, several spectrums and sliders are available online to help guide the process.

For example, your brand's personality could be on various points of a spectrum for each of these areas:

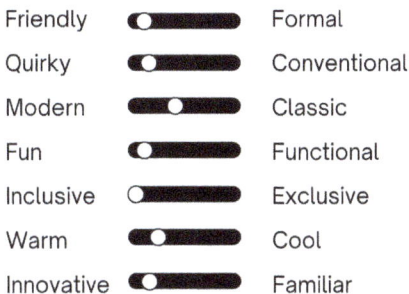

Friendly	Formal
Quirky	Conventional
Modern	Classic
Fun	Functional
Inclusive	Exclusive
Warm	Cool
Innovative	Familiar

In addition to using color theory to select a color palette, color psychology is used to elicit a specific emotional response to a brand—like trust, adventure, safety, or urgency. *Chapter 13: Color Meanings* includes a summary of emotions associated with various colors.

Although there are variations, here are some color generalizations by industry:

- The retail industry uses red to stimulate energy and excitement as well as influence impulse purchases.
- The healthcare and pharmaceutical industry uses blue to convey trust, reliability, and a sense of calm.
- The technology sector uses blue to convey trust, competence, and intelligence.
- In the food and beverage industry:
    - Fast food uses red, orange, and yellow to increase hunger.
    - Healthy food uses green to convey fresh, organic, and natural.
- The fashion industry uses black for sophistication, power, and glamor.

Confetti Dreamers

This is the color palette for Confetti Dreamers:

| Confetti Dreamers
| Confetti Dreamers
| Confetti Dreamers
| Confetti Dreamers
| Confetti Dreamers
| Confetti Dreamers
| Confetti Dreamers
| Confetti Dreamers

© Confetti Dream Publishing, LLC 2024

It had to embrace color, *right?*

The personality traits for the Confetti Dreamers brand:

- accepting/belonging
- creative
- quirky
- inspired
- joyful

You will read more about Confetti Dreamers in Part Two.

Chapter 12

Everything (Anything) on a Spectrum

If you think about it, all of life can be translated into spectrums, ranges, or distributions of something. Some spectrums function like a gauge, such as a gas gauge, where left is empty and right is full. Other spectrums are used to organize or cluster similar items together.

Familiar Spectrums

As we know, color is literally a spectrum of light waves, with each color equating to its wavelength in nanometers.[18]

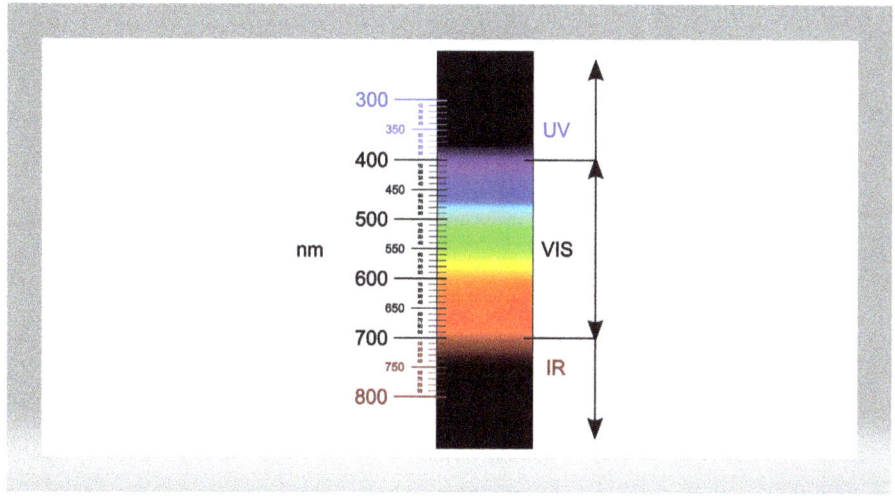

Other commonly known "spectrums" include the political spectrum and the homelessness spectrum.

Here's what they might look like.

Using terminology from the Pew Research Center (2021), this is one way to represent a spectrum of political ideologies in the United States. It shows the range from **conservative** to **progressive** and conveys partisan polarization. However, it does not begin to capture the range of issues and variations of opinions within each ideology.

---

[18] "Light spectrum (precise colors).svg" by Fulvio314 CC BY-SA 4.0

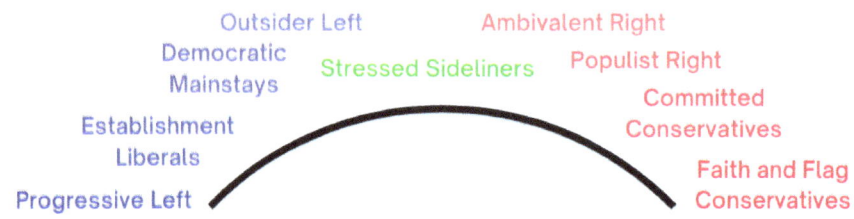

Political Spectrum

Using terminology from the National Alliance to End Homelessness (2024), this spectrum attempts to represent the various states of homelessness (also referred to as houselessness or being unhoused). From unsheltered to permanent housing, these terms capture different stages of the homelessness experience.

Homelessness Spectrum

Other Spectrums

New spectrums can be created by taking a topic and arranging its subtopics on a spectrum.

This first example is music genres, loosely grouped by similarities. A person might enjoy a wide variety of music genres across the spectrum or perhaps a cluster of similar styles.

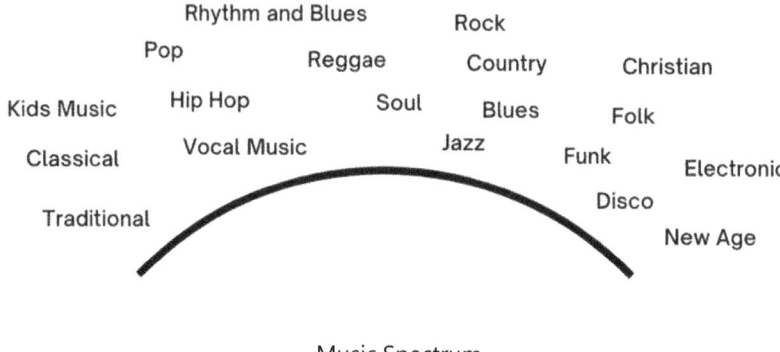

Music Spectrum

This feelings spectrum shows a range of emotions used to describe specific life experiences. Negative feelings are on the left, and positive feelings are on the right.

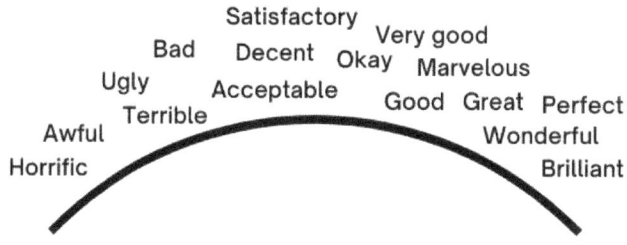

Feelings Spectrum

Spectrums are threaded throughout this book as reminders of the gradients in our worlds.

Chapter 13

Spectrums of Color Meanings

The following spectrums summarize the emotions associated with certain colors as defined by color psychologists. The words have been organized (chunked) to show relationships within a range. Because each of us is unique, these descriptions are neither universally true nor complete.

Red is a warm, powerful color.

Orange is associated with autumn, citrus, thinking, talking, fun, and also stimulates the appetite.

Yellow is associated with sunshine and is the first color the eye notices.

Green is associated with the natural environment and is the easiest color on the eyes.

Blue is a relaxing color associated with the sea and sky.

Violet (purple) is associated with royalty, spirituality, and can also influence the imagination.

Pinks are high tint reds that convey femininity, innocence, and optimism.

Turquoise is a friendly, happy color. Teal is a more sophisticated version of turquoise and is often associated with trust and reliability.

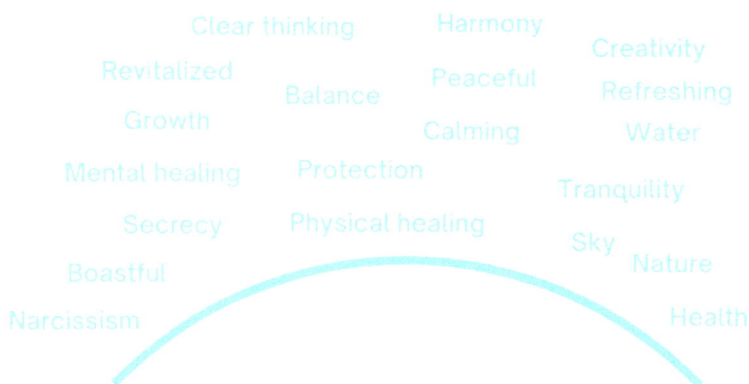

Black is associated with darkness—night, death, and evil—as well as timeless sophistication.

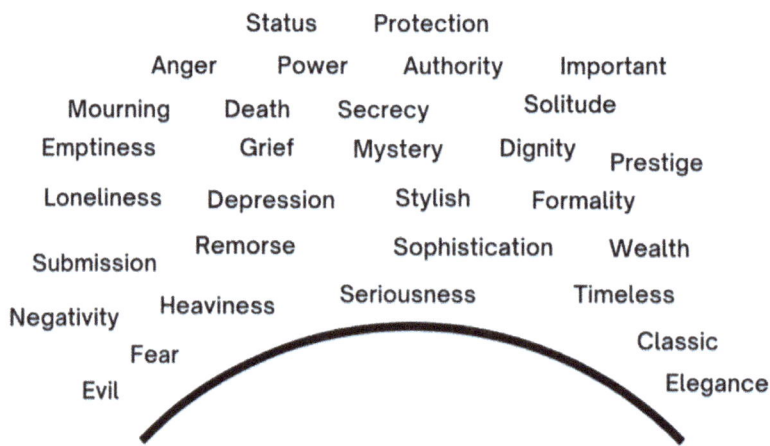

White is associated with light and purity.

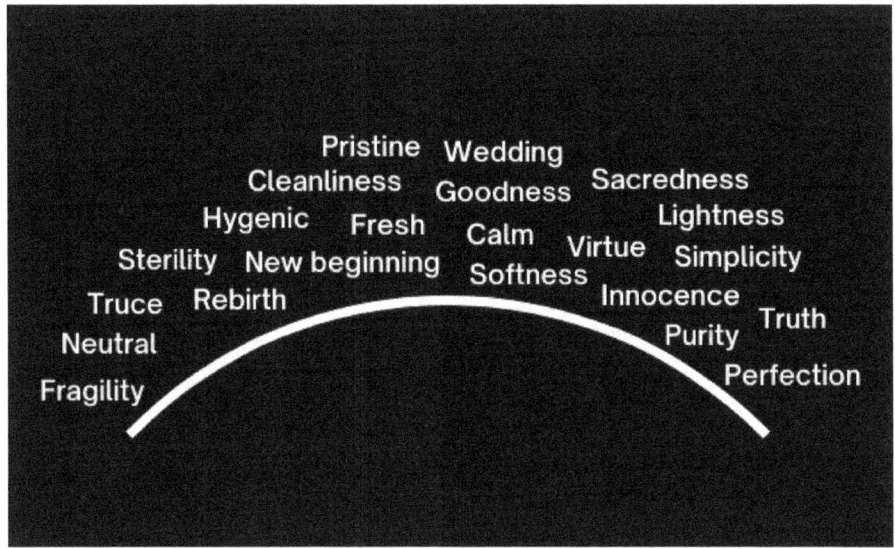

Grays are less emotional than other colors and can represent neutrality, indecision, and compromise.

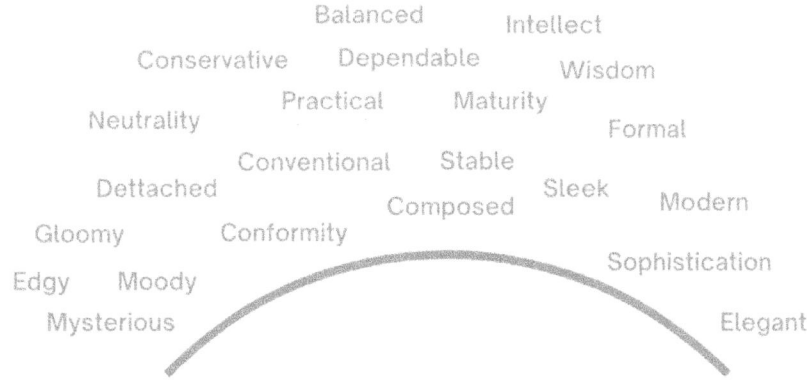

Brown provides a sense of safety and security.

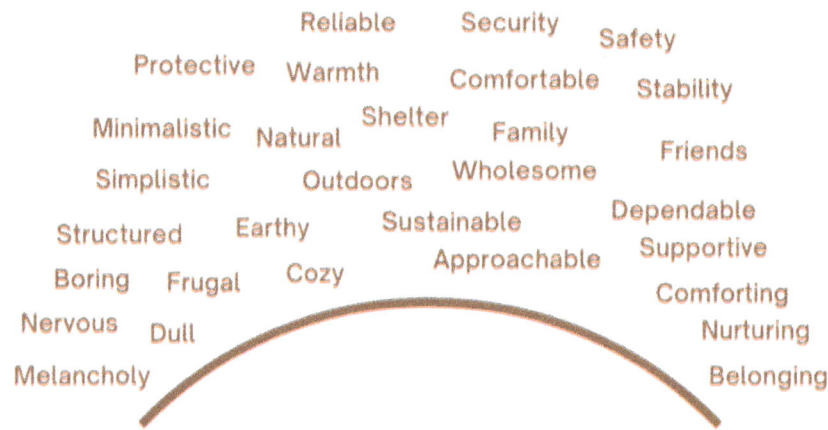

Silver illuminates and reflects, giving it a fluid quality.

Gold is associated with wealth, success, and status.

There is a plethora of information online about color psychology. One of my favorites is *Empowered by Color*.[19]

As conveyed in the color spectrums, colors are associated with various adjectives, traits, moods, or brands. Some color meanings are universal, while others seem to contradict each other. That's how color works. It's part science, part art.

---

[19] https://www.empower-yourself-with-color-psychology.com/

Chapter 14

Cultural Color Meanings

Although there are common meanings associated with specific colors, these can vary by location. The following list shows how culture, as an environmental factor, can impact a person's perceptions and reactions to color.

Luck:

- Green: Ireland
- Red: China
- Orange: China
- Gold: China (especially in weddings)
- Teal/turquoise: Australia

Marriage:

- Red: Most of Asia
- White: Western countries (white for brides)
- Vibrant reds, pinks, oranges, or greens: India

Death or mourning:

- Dark red: Ivory Coast in Africa
- Red: South Africa
- Yellow: Egypt
- Blue: Iran
- Purple: Latin America, widows in Thailand
- Black: Middle East, South America, Western countries
- White: Italy, Japan, China, Eastern countries

Masculine:

- Red: France
- Blue: Most of the world
- Light blue: United States (little boys)

Feminine:

- Blue: China (little girls)
- Pink: United States (little girls)

It's important to be aware of cultural meanings because they can influence or override color psychology.

Chapter 15

Rainbows

Sometimes a rainbow of colors or a literal rainbow is the best way to represent how you feel. When I experience surges of positivity from being inspired, productive, creative, understood, or innovative, I also feel an explosion of rainbow colors. Do you ever 'feel' the rainbow too?

Symbolism

Rainbows are unique and special, symbolizing hope, optimism, and promises of good things to come. They represent beauty, celebration, and joy. Double rainbows, considered doubly good, are signs of abundance and balance, resonating with a lover's embrace or soulmates. No wonder rainbows are used in so many places; they radiate positivity.

Rainbows also have religious meanings:

- In Christianity and Judaism, rainbows symbolize blessings and faith in God's promises.
- In Hinduism, each chakra (an energy center in the body) is represented by a color of the rainbow.

- In Buddhism, the "rainbow body" represents the five cosmic elements of space, air, fire, water, and earth.
- In Ancient Norse and for Native Americans, rainbows symbolize a bridge for spirits and deities between realms.

I think the spectrum of meanings associated with rainbows reflects the diversity of our world.

Embrace the Rainbow as 'More Than'

The rainbow now represents even more as it is used to help people engage in diversity and inclusivity, words that evoke a wonderfully welcoming embrace for everyone.

A bit of history...

Gilbert Baker created the Rainbow Flag in 1978 as an act of social justice to show unity and support for gays, lesbians, bisexuals, and transgender individuals (Baker, 2021). His bold actions sparked a movement, and since then, the Rainbow Flag has evolved to become the international **symbol for acceptance, justice, and equality for all**.

While some people have expressed frustration with what they view as contradictory meanings of the rainbow—the religious and LGBTQIA+ meanings, respectively—they absolutely can coexist. It doesn't have to be one or the other; it can be both. Showing kindness and compassion to all, regardless of their identity, is a wonderful way to carry out the commandment to "love thy neighbor" (Leviticus 19:18, NIV; Mark 12:30-31, NIV).

As with everything, meanings and trends ebb and flow. A rainbow of colors is embraced by many companies: Peacock TV©, NBC Universal©, Google©, and more.

I encourage everyone to accept the rainbow as a beautiful expression of color and belonging. If you're not there yet, then perhaps a metamorphosis awaits you in your future.[20]

[20] Adobe Firefly prompt: "rainbow butterfly realistic and colorful rainbow butterfly with confetti isolated on white"

Part Two

An Enlightening Adventure into the World of Neurodiversity and Autism

Chapter 16

Color and Neurodiversity

Surprise! This wouldn't be the first time my neurodivergent brain appears to jump to an unrelated topic. Switching from color to neurodiversity may seem like a stretch, but from my perspective, there is a clear connection.

To help connect the dots, download your free guide from ConfettiDreamers.com/Autism.

Could this squirrel-like thought process be my superpower?[21]

I recently learned about orthogonality. It is "the process of drawing from a variety of perhaps seemingly unrelated perspectives to achieve new insights; can be considered a strength of Autistic minds" (Reframing Autism, 2024). Hmmm. I think I like it.

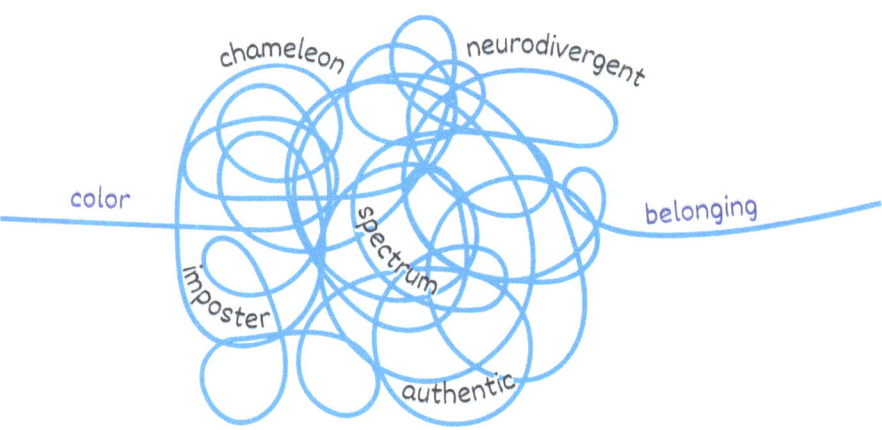

What's the Connection?

Simply put, the common thread connecting Parts One and Two is **spectrum.**[22]

- This book starts with the color spectrum.
- Now it continues with spectrums of neurodiversity and belonging.
  - Belonging? Yes...

---

[21] © "Messy Lines Finding Solution" by Canva creator sergeyparanchuk 2024
[22] © "Venn Diagram Three Circles Overlapping" by Canva creator Mystikal Forest 2024

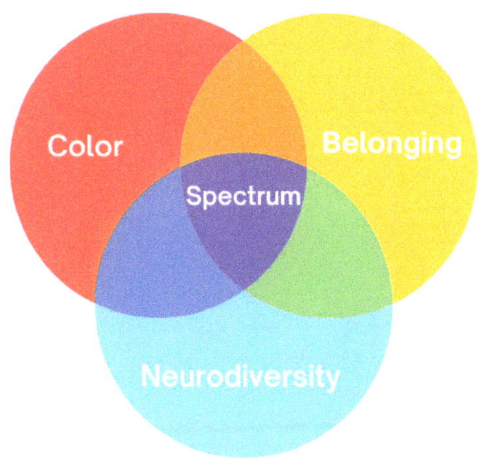

What Color Are You?

"My favorite color is you."

This is a line from AJR's song, *"Sober Up."* I discovered the band a few years ago and fell in love with their quirky, smart, and authentic lyrics. Their playful words roll off their tongues like a story, flecked with hints of imposter syndrome, messy lives, and conflicting priorities. *"Sober Up"* initially sounds like a song about drinking, but there's a deeper message. The lead singer, Jack, looks to his authentic self from childhood to help him sober up from the "weight of being an adult" (Strydom, 2018). "My favorite color is you"—is your authentic self from when you were young.

What Color Is Your Authentic Self?

Your authentic self is who you are when no one is watching—when you are carefree and uninhibited.

From these statements, which one fits you the best?

- Your true colors were most vibrant as a carefree youth.
- You are just starting to embrace your authentic self.

- You are still trying to find your true colors.
- You are living a colorfully authentic life.

According to **Maslow's Hierarchy of Needs**, a sense of belonging is critical for your mental health and quality of life. (●●●)

© Plateresca 2017

The following **Spectrum of Belonging** describes how you might feel in certain situations or times in your life. The statement you selected above, about the color of your authentic self, may relate to your sense of belonging.

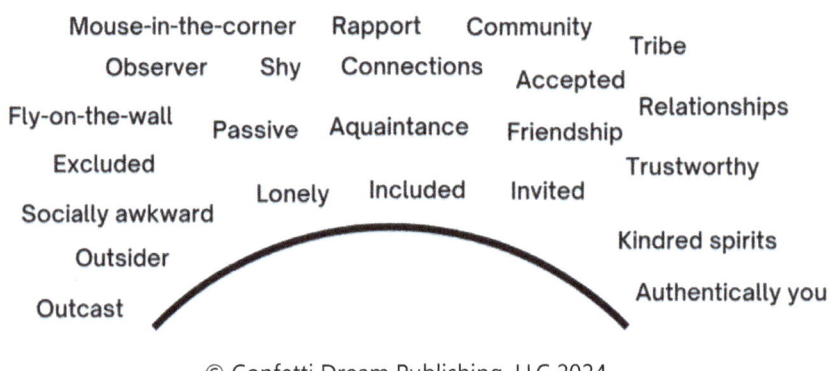

© Confetti Dream Publishing, LLC 2024

Embrace Your True Colors

I have been various colors throughout my life, oftentimes correlating to my sense of belonging:

- The palest of pale as the timid one in the corner.
- Black as a kindergartener, perhaps because of my controlled energy.
- Bright yellow and aqua when living at the pool as a child, convinced I was a mermaid.
- An ombre of color, growing brighter with experience, skills, and confidence.
- A chameleon, quickly changing my colors to please others, morphing to a pale grayish yellow when not getting it right.
- Shades of red when embarrassed, particularly a deep red when feeling like an imposter.
- Somber colors of inky black and gray when experiencing intense grief of loss and death.
- An explosive confetti of colors when celebrating and overjoyed—walking down the aisle, the birth of my daughters, and graduating with my master's degree.
- Glittery and sparkly colors when I share my passion with others.
- A dainty white when my gentle soul feels so rare and delicate but is somehow valued by others.

My sincere hope for all of us is to embrace our true colors and live authentically.

To get from here to there, let's look at neurodiversity and see if there really is a connection between these seemingly disparate parts.

Neurodiversity

As mentioned in the prologue, "**neurodiversity** refers to the diversity of human minds and all the unique and different ways that people can exist, think, act, process, feel, and function" (Wise, 2024).

Neurodivergence is relative to what is considered "neuro-normative" (that is, a social construct created and accepted by society) that means:

- The closer a person is to the majority agreed-upon normal range of neurological and behavioral functioning, the more **neurotypical** they would be considered.
- Hypothetically speaking (ignoring other systemic factors), a **neurotypical** person would experience fewer barriers to accessing basic necessities within their community, such as housing, education, employment, public spaces, healthcare, and medication.

Neurodivergent is an umbrella term that categorizes neurological differences that 'diverge' from the range of 'normal' (i.e., neuro-normativity). These differences include both innate and acquired divergences.

From Reframing Autism, these are examples of some neurological differences (and their diagnostic labels):

- innate (e.g., Autism) or acquired (e.g., brain injury)
- medical conditions (e.g., epilepsy)
- mental health conditions (e.g., trauma)
- learning disabilities (e.g., dyslexia)
- other neurodevelopmental conditions (e.g., ADHD)

Divergence from the "agreed normal"—as defined by the Diagnostic and Statistical Manual of Mental Disorders (DSM) and societal expectations—tends to result in more difficulties for the individual.

The challenges neurodivergent people face are both:

- organic to the differences in their brain
- the result of societal design

Living in a world designed for neurotypical brains is considered the primary barrier to the social model of disability, which focuses on our *disabling world* instead of *disabled people*.

The terms neurodivergent and neurotypical can help us differentiate how one's brain processes and responds to input from the five senses—sight, sound, taste, touch, and smell. Sensory processing is one of the ways Autistic people have divergent experiences.

Despite my love of words, for some reason my brain struggles to correctly use the terms neurodiversity, neurodiverse, and neurodivergent. If you can relate to this, I recommend checking out *Neuroqueer, The Writings of Dr. Nick Walker* (2023).

The Spectrum of Neurodiversity

The following image shows what neurodiversity can include (Middleton et al, 2024; Elsherif et al., 2022).[23]

Notes about this image:

- it includes "neurotypicality"
- many of these diagnoses can co-occur (and often do)
- it does not reflect all aspects or expressions of neurodiversity

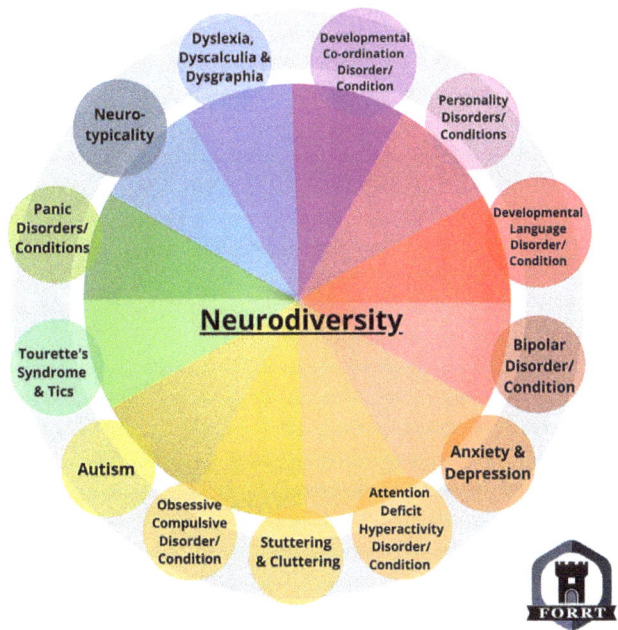

Used with permission from FORRT > Framework for Open and Reproducible Research Training @ 2023 CC BY-NC-SA 4.0

---

[23] Elsherif et al., 2022 https://doi.org/10.31222/osf.io/k7a9p

As you can see, neurodiversity includes numerous diagnostic labels. Because of my personal experience and wanting to spread the word with others, the rest of the book focuses on Autism Spectrum Disorder (ASD).

Chapter 17

Autism

Let's look at Autism, partly because it is on a spectrum, **and** more importantly, because diagnoses are on the rise and there is a huge opportunity to learn more, especially for women.

The Autism Spectrum Difference is explained by Embrace Autism as, "A neurodevelopmental difference characterized by alterations in social functioning, hypersensitivity to stimuli, repetitive behaviors, and deep interests—often combined with advanced cognitive and perceptive abilities."

Early Days of Autism

Research on Autism in children, specifically boys, is documented from the early 1900s, with initial studies focusing more on extreme cases. As more data became available in the second half of the twentieth century, the scope of the Autistic "spectrum" widened. A search on "Autism in children" results in a plethora of information on definitions, signs, symptoms, causes, treatments, and education.

Asperger Syndrome was recognized as a distinct subtype of Autistic Disorder and included in the DSM-IV in 1994. The diagnostic criteria are similar to those for Autistic Disorder but include "typical language development, average cognitive abilities, and average adaptive behavior abilities (other than in social interaction)." At this point, clinicians and researchers began to conceptualize Autism along a broad continuum or spectrum of functioning levels and abilities (May et al., 2016).

Asperger Syndrome was eliminated with the publication of the DSM-5 (APA, 2013) and reclassified within the Autism Spectrum Disorder diagnosis, specifically ASD-1. Many people who met the criteria for Asperger's Disorder would now meet the criteria for Autism Spectrum Disorder with a Level 1 severity qualifier (ASD-Level 1) (May et al.). The term remains controversial because of Hans Asperger's ties to Nazi Germany (Sheffer, 2018). Many within the Autistic community still strongly affiliate with the diagnostic title of Asperger's and identify as "Aspies" (Flowers et al., 2023). Others consider the term elitist and divisive to the community, as it signifies that there are "better and more useful" Autists (Murray, 2023).

Why Autistic Women+?

Capital A

You probably noticed the use of a capital 'A' for Autism, Autistic, and Autist. This is an intentional choice to show respect for the Autistic community. The purpose is to reclaim the term from the medical/pathology model, similar to how the Deaf community has reclaimed their term as a source of positive identity and culture (Benham and Kizer, 2016; Weller, 2023).

Identity-first Language

To align with the expressed preference of the Autistic community, I use identity-first language (instead of person-first language) (Keating et al., 2022; Taboas et al., 2023).

- **Identity-first: "Autistic woman"**
- Person-first: "woman with Autism"

I acknowledge and respect that some Autistic individuals may prefer alternate terms.

Inclusivity

The plus (+) in the Facebook Group Autistic Women+ Living Authentically is significant because it conveys the inclusivity and authenticity of the community.

When you're being authentic, you may not always color inside the lines. Having a safe space allows us to learn from each other, start to unmask, and show our true colors. When we truly listen to each other **with** compassion and *without* judgment, **the world becomes a magical place.**

From the Facebook group's About page: "[The group] aims to provide a safe and supportive space for authentic Autistic expression where we may share stories, seek and offer support, exchange ideas and resources, and find validation and camaraderie among our peers."

Research shows that more diversity exists in the Autistic community regarding sexual orientation and gender identity. For example, Warrier et al. (2021) found that transgender and genderqueer adults were three to six times more likely to be diagnosed as Autistic than cisgender adults. Personally, I identify as a heterosexual cisgender female, which means someone who was assigned female at birth (AFAB) and is attracted to the opposite sex (male). *"Cisgender" specifically means that gender identity corresponds with the sex assigned at birth.* I know people who experience gender discomfort, where their soul doesn't match their physical body. With empathy, I have made a conscientious effort to educate myself in this area. My intent is not to politicize it, but to bring awareness and compassion.

To encourage authenticity and center inclusivity, the Facebook Group is for Autistic people who (gender) identify as:

- Women: assigned female at birth
- Trans (AMAB/AFAB): assigned male at birth, identify as female / assigned female at birth, identify as male
- Non-binary
- Gender fluid
- Agender

Autism in Women+

In the past twenty years, the diagnosis of Autism has grown significantly—upwards of 787 percent between 1998 and 2018—with the greatest rise among adults (Neuroscience News, 2021). This surge relates to an evolved, more inclusive definition. With an increase in awareness of Autism by various organizations and policy changes related to adult assessment, the updated, "Autism narrative [is something] that many women and girls identify with" (Neuroscience News, 2021).

Often, undiagnosed women who feel burned out from heavy masking are desperate for answers to questions like, "Why is life so difficult?" and "Why don't I fit in?" As awareness continues to expand, people are beginning to discover a greater support network and pool of resources to help them move from survival to stability. For women who are aware and curious, tools for self-evaluation and self-identification are more readily available. Additionally, information about Autism is more accessible in a variety of spaces—from fiction books with neurodivergent characters to stories and documentaries, and from YouTube channels to support groups. For some, media and social media can play a significant role in a journey of Autistic self-discovery.

While there are initiatives around Autism education, there is a clear need for educating and re-educating in this space using updated inclusive terminology, research on adult women, workplace accommodations, and guidance for general practitioners and mental health providers. For example, simple modifications to communication methods and environments can have a positive impact on Autistic women+, as well as usable tools such as appointment preparation tips, information on a person's rights in healthcare, credible medical information, and follow-up accountability aids (Nicolaidis et al., 2015). In the meantime, for women who go undiagnosed or are mistreated due to a lack of qualified medical training, the damages are real and deep.

Masking

Masking, known as social camouflaging, is when a neurodivergent person mimics a neurotypical person in an attempt to fit in (assimilate) and build connections with others (Hull et al., 2017). Ah, another reference to belonging and safety. (●●●) Females are much more inclined to mask than males, and they can be quite adept. In fact, they can be so convincing that they go undiagnosed or misdiagnosed.

Please note, masking is not exclusive to Autistic females. Others engage in ongoing aligning with majority normal masking, resulting in detrimental effects on mental health—including non-stereotypically presenting Autistic males, non-binary and gender-diverse individuals, people with other neurodivergent traits, as well as minority cultural groups and non-heteronormative groups (Price, 2022; Pearson & Rose, 2021; Hull et al., 2017).

But years of constant efforts to mask can take its toll—emotionally, physically, socially, and behaviorally. Neurodivergent Autistic women+ have reported feeling rejected, isolated, lonely, desperate, and exhausted (Hull et al.). Autistic women+ who go undiagnosed can suffer from numerous co-occurring conditions, including depression, grief from not being accepted, anxiety and exhaustion from the weight of trying to fit in, obsessive-compulsive behavior as they attempt to control plans, sensory sensitivities and sensory overload, meltdowns, shutdowns, and more (Milner et al., 2018). This list sounds familiar...

The Autism Spectrum | Many Visual Representations

The Autism spectrum is now common terminology, but the "Autism" and "spectrum" parts are often misunderstood.

The Autism spectrum is **not** this type of range—from "not Autistic" to "Autistic": [24]

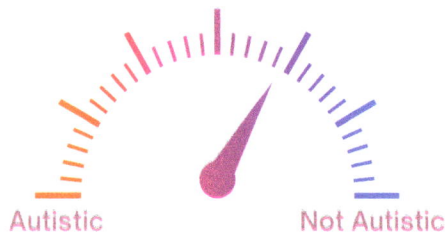

Instead, the spectrum encompasses the range of highs and lows in several areas—language, motor skills, sensory filter, executive function, and perception. Autists (people with Autism) have a range of skills (low-mid-high) that may require a range of support (low-mid-high) in these areas.

The Autism spectrum could look like this **spectrum of mini spectrums.**

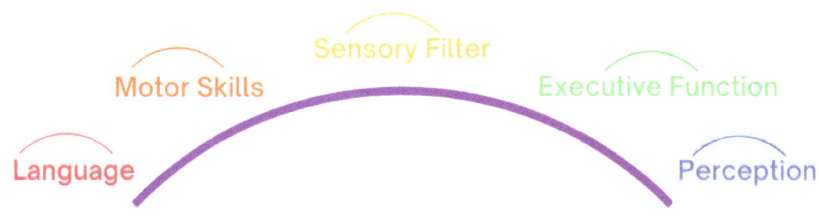

© Confetti Dream Publishing, LLC 2024

For each area (mini rainbow), envision a label identifying skills as low, mid, or high. Considering all the five-dot combinations underscores this truth: every individual on the spectrum is unique. Just as we perceive color differently, no one on the Autism spectrum is exactly like another person on the Autism spectrum.

---

[24] © "Speedometer Gauge Icon" by Canva creator musmellow 2024

This **circular Autism Spectrum** conveys a similar concept in a circle (Exclusive Says, n.d.). To experiment with different combinations, check out this interactive Autism Spectrum online.[25]

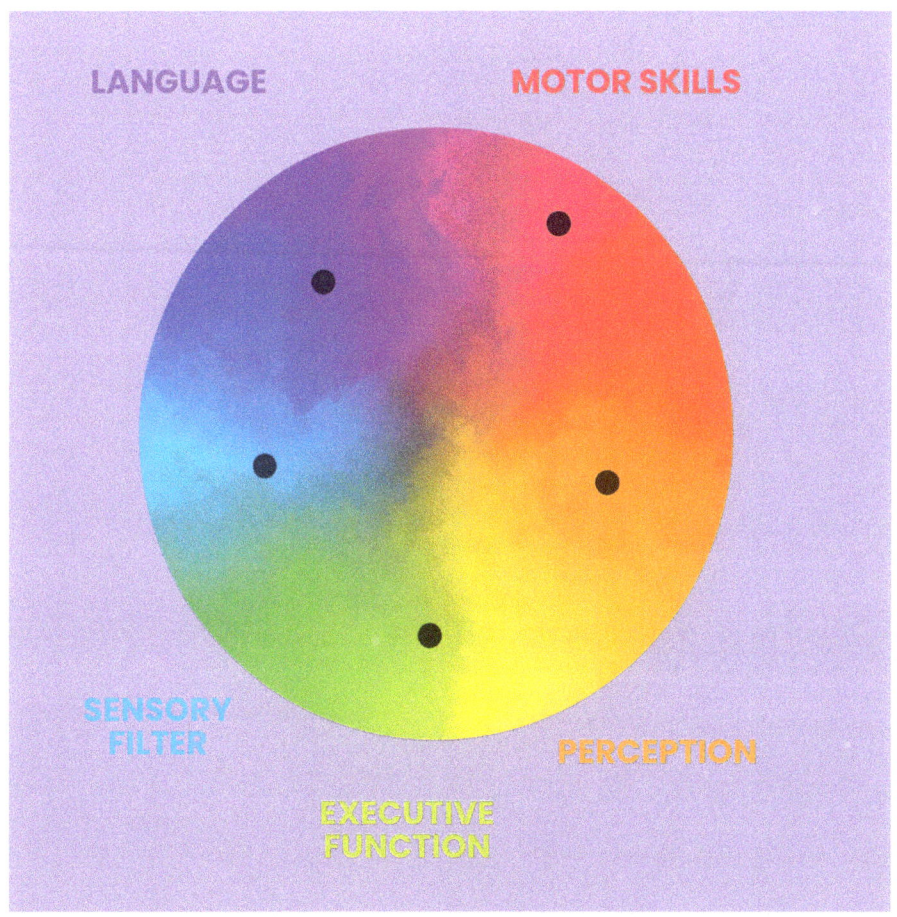

Note: *I tried desperately to uncover who created this web page, to no avail. If this is yours, I'd love to hear from you.*

---

[25] https://exclusive.says.com/my/exclusive/what-is-Autism-a-simple-guide-to-understanding-the-spectrum/index.html

Continuing with the theme of a circle, this **Wheel of Autism** by Lyric Rivera includes "vast and varied shades (sensory & motor, emotional & cognitive, communication & social, dependency on routine & aversion to surprises)" (Rivera, 2023).

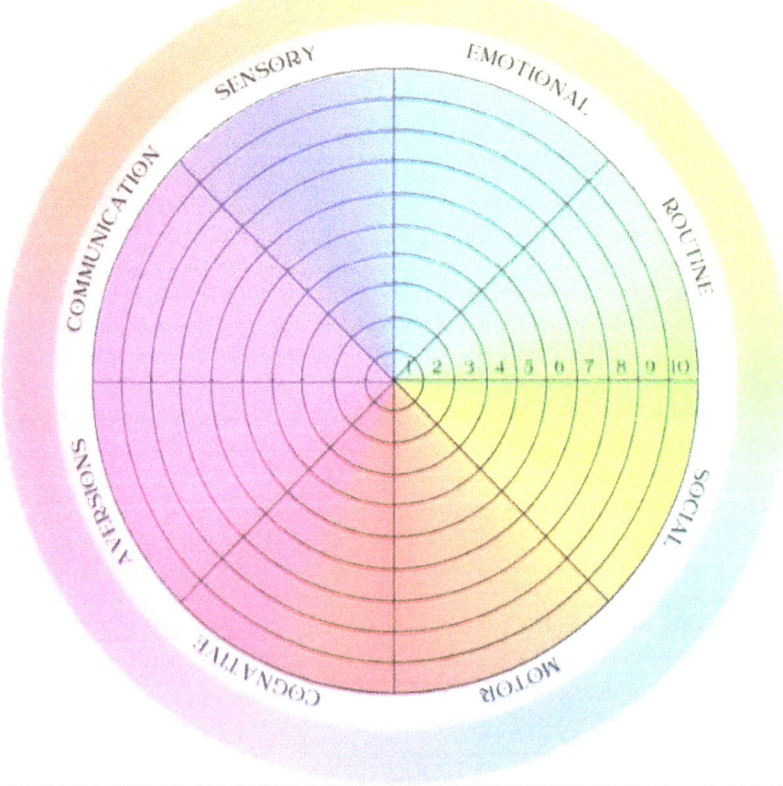

Used with permission © Neurodivergent Rebel, Neurodivergent Consulting 2023

The **Adaptive Therapy for Autistic Adults (ATAA®) Autism Wheel©** by Claire Jack[26] is another wheel designed to reflect the diversity of your personal experiences. A higher score points towards Autistic behavior, but is not necessarily negative (e.g., stimming you find soothing).

For each category, rate yourself on a scale of 1 to 10.

- 1 = does not affect you at all
- 2–8 = affects you to some degree (2 = less severe; 9 = more intense)
- 10 = severely impacts you or you engage in it to a high degree

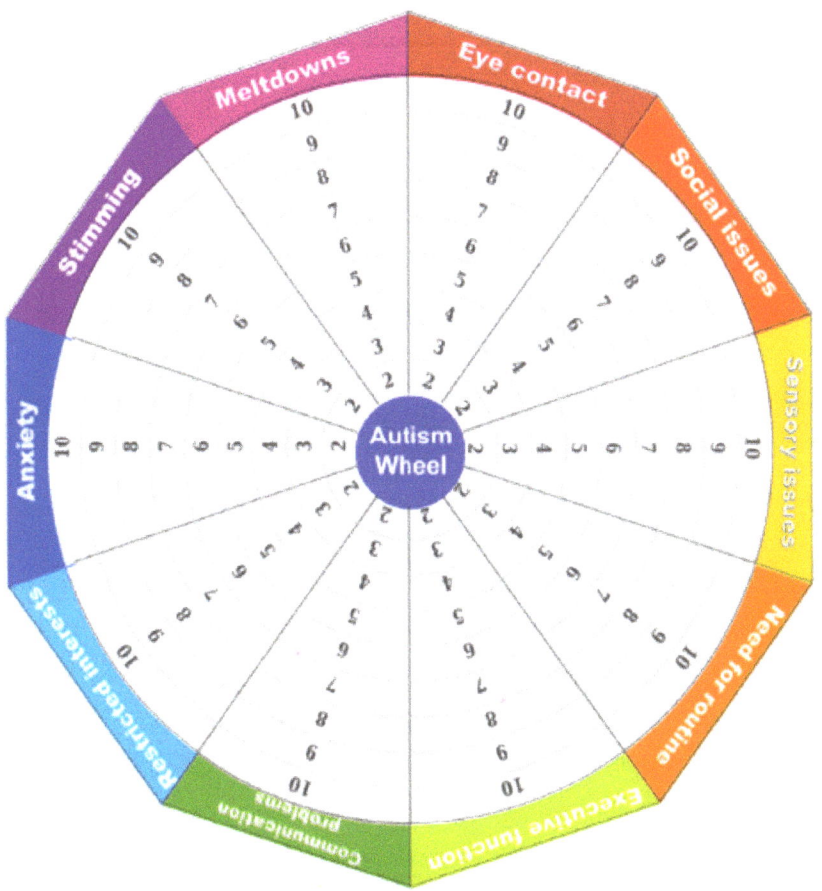

Used with permission © Claire Jack, Ph.D., 2023

---

[26] https://www.facebook.com/drclairejack/

Finally, here's yet another way to visually convey the Autism spectrum (Lynch, 2019).[27] In this **linear version**, there are variations in how Autism manifests in each of these seven areas: pragmatic language, social awareness, monotropic mindset, information processing, sensory processing, repetitive behaviors, and neuromotor differences. In this graphic, the variations impact the color intensity on the spectrum.

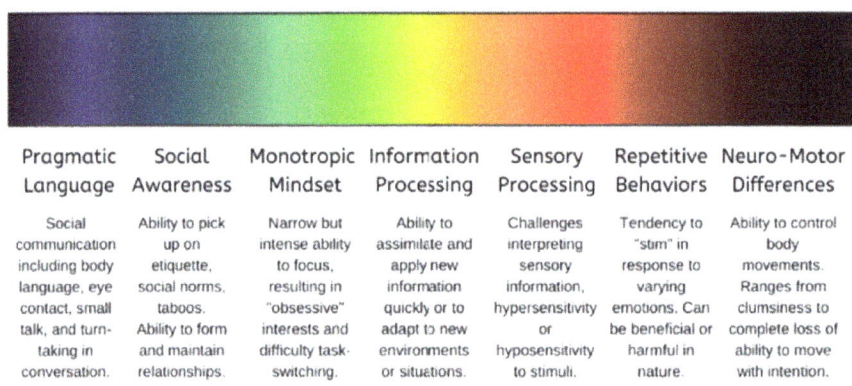

Used with permission © C.L. Lynch 2019

Key takeaway: there are many ways to visually represent the Autism spectrum.

While the Autism spectrum is not a range of "not Autistic" to "Autistic," it's important to note that a formal diagnosis of Autistic Spectrum Disorder (ASD) includes the level of support as part of the diagnosis:

- ASD-1 = Level 1 = Requiring some support
- ASD-2 = Level 2 = Requiring substantial support
- ASD-3 = Level 3 = Requiring very substantial support

Functioning levels are a source of contention because of their discriminatory effects and inaccurate representations of an Autist's actual functioning, which fluctuates depending on multiple factors and contexts. Those classified as Level 1 often have their support needs denied, while those with

---

[27] https://neuroclastic.com/its-a-spectrum-doesnt-mean-what-you-think

Level 3 are denied autonomy and presumed incompetent. Additionally, the level of support specifier is often assigned based on intelligence and language ability, even though intellectual impairment and language disability are not part of the diagnostic criteria for ASD (ASAN, 2021).

What if your skills are mostly high? Is this why some people say, "Everybody is a little Autistic"?

This statement is becoming more common and may be related to an increased awareness of Autism without fully understanding the nuances.

It may seem like a harmless statement, but it is quite hurtful and undermining for someone whose life is challenged every day. Although these types of insensitive statements may come from a place of unfamiliarity or curiosity, making light of a diagnosis can be triggering and a potential deal-breaker for some Autistic people (Captain Quirk, 2017).

As awareness of ASD increases, my hope is for conversations about Autism to become more mainstream. While it's not your responsibility to educate others, there are ways to respond that encourage growth and empathy. After all, it's not surprising to meet people who can identify with Autistic traits and who may also be interested in learning more. (●●●)

Autistic Traits

The following list comprises traits related to the Autism spectrum. The purpose for sharing this is to show the wide range of traits; it is not meant to be a complete list. For each area, a person could have a low, mid, or high level of skills impacting what supports (low, mid, high), if any, are needed. A few skills contradict each other, which reflects the uniqueness in how Autism presents itself. Remember, there is no one-size-fits-all.

Note: The terms dyspraxia and synesthesia are defined in more detail after the table. (●●●)

Autistic Traits by Area

This table translates my interpretation of how you could map traits of ASD from the Embrace Autism website (Engelbrecht & Silvertant, 2024) to the five categories, along with additional traits from other sources.

Area	Strengths	Challenges
• Language	• Giftedness • Encyclopedia knowledge	• Dyspraxia, Apraxia: speech difficulties • Repetition of words or phrases • Stilted or scripted speech

• Motor	• None noted	• Abnormal gait
		• Dyspraxia, Apraxia:
		  ○ Clumsiness
		  ○ Poor balance
		  ○ Poor eye-hand coordination
		  ○ Poor handwriting
		  ○ Poor posture
		• Repetitive behaviors (hand flapping, rocking, spinning)

• Sensory	• Acute hearing
	  ○ Heightened pitch detection
	  ○ Superior auditory discrimination
	• Enhanced olfactory detection
	  ○ Smell, sound, taste
	• Synesthesia (2+ senses at once)
	• Increased adaptive coding (facial recognition)
		• Diminished adaptive coding (facial recognition)
		• Fear response to calm chemicals
		• Overwhelm, meltdowns, shutdowns
		• Sensory sensitivity/hypersensitivity (e.g., bright lights, strong smells, textured fabrics, loud noises)
		• Sensory overload

• Executive Function	• Lateral thinking • Powerful memory • Rational decision-making • Strong work ethic • Superior problem solving	• Active resting network (switch does not fire up or turn off) • Aversion to maintaining eye contact • Difficulty making and keeping friends • Difficulty regulating emotions • Dyspraxia, Apraxia: disorganized • Excessive daydreaming • High prevalence of PTSD • Literal interpretation of abstract ideas • Low self-esteem • Low theory of mind (misread emotions, intentions, or cues) • Obsessive interests

Area	Strengths	Challenges
		• Restricted interests • Rigid/inflexible thinking and behavior (hard to cope with change) • Rumination (excessive, repetitive thinking about an event) • Sleep problems; fatigue
• Perception	• Color intensity and perception • Detail-oriented • Extraordinary vision • Sharp gradient of spatial attention • Optical illusions • Pattern recognition • Tunnel vision • Visual hypersensitivity	• Alexithymia co-occurrence (difficulty identifying, recognizing, and describing emotions) • Arranging things in a particular manner • Forgetting faces • Hyperacusis (loud noises cause pain) • Lack of proficiency with use of non-verbal gestures

Do you relate to some of these traits?

Many people relate to some of the traits, or maybe many of them. Later, I will share some resources if you are interested in learning more about your brain and how it works. (●●●)

Some Co-occurring Conditions

With Autism, traits or characteristics can overlap between co-occurring conditions. While it is not my intention to explain all the similarities and differences, having an awareness is important because it helps you make connections and provides some context for your potential next steps.

Autism, ADHD, and Dyspraxia

The following diagram shows how three common co-occurrences are similar and different: Autism, ADHD, and Dyspraxia.[28]

Each diagnosis has components related to motor skills:

- ADHD presents with hyperactivity.
- Dyspraxia relates to coordination and speech difficulties.

As you can see, the **spectrum of traits** includes more than motor skills.

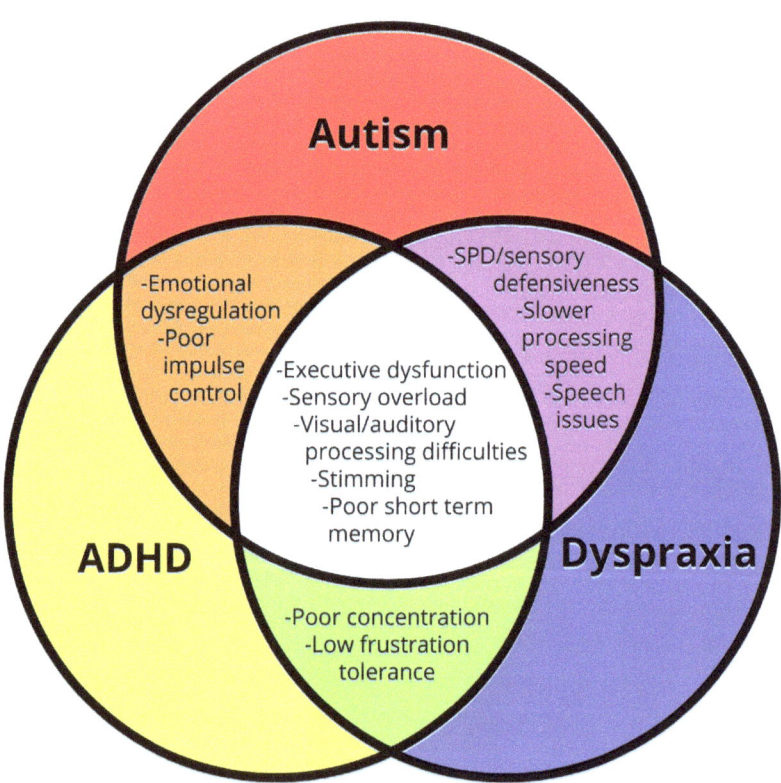

If you relate to some of these characteristics, you may start to better understand how your brain makes sense of and interacts with the world.

---

[28] ActuallyDyspraxic on Tumblr

Synesthesia

Did you know some people experience one sense through another sense—or two senses simultaneously? Amazing!

Examples of synesthesia:

- See or hear a word and taste food
- Hear sounds and see shapes or patterns
- Feel an object with your hands and hear a sound

Examples synesthesia related to color:

- Hear a name and see a color
- See a specific color for each day of the week
- See color when playing music (e.g., melody as shapes, chords as colors)

Several famous musicians see color when they play music. For example, Mickey Hart, the drummer for the Grateful Dead, sees color when he plays. He literally creates a visually artistic piece when drumming, allowing him to play "outside the box" of traditional drumming rules (Baldani, n.d.).

When I first heard of the concept of synesthesia, it blew me away.

When I have a hard time wrapping my head around something, I try to come up with a similar example I can relate to or apply to myself. For example, I have a hypersensitivity to lavender—natural or synthetic. I also sneeze whenever I have a peppermint lozenge. This may be hard for some to understand, but for me, it's reality.

What if synesthesia is their "lavender" or their "peppermint"?

But why do I share this?

For one, synesthesia **manifesting as color** for some individuals is so relevant.

It's also a gentle reminder that there is no right or wrong way to experience this world. Considering others' experiences and being sensitive to them helps build empathy and compassion.

Chapter 18

Signs of Stress and Its Effects

Stress is particularly common for people who are caught in a cycle of wondering why they feel so different from the rest of the world and constantly mask as they attempt to fit into social norms. Stress is your body's reaction to harmful situations, regardless of whether the harm is real or perceived.

Effects of Stress

Stress causes your nervous system to kick into gear by activating your fight-or-flight response. Your heart rate and blood pressure increase, your muscles tighten, and your breathing quickens as your body releases cortisol, a stress hormone, in preparation to fight danger or flee the situation. "Back in the day," caveman stress was critically important because it translated to life or death. Unfortunately, the list of stressors has increased in modern times, **and** our fight-or-flight response remains as strong as ever. Prolonged exposure to stress can damage your body.

Everyone's list of stressors is unique. What causes me to stress out may have little to no impact on you, and vice versa.

Not sure if your levels of stress are healthy or are causing distress?

Here are some signs of unhealthy stress:

- Emotionally, stress can cause you to become agitated, overwhelmed, moody, and depressed.
- Physically, stress can show up as insomnia, fatigue, headaches, digestive issues, chest pain, frequent illnesses, nervousness, clenched jaw, or grinding of teeth.
- Cognitively, stress may present itself through worry, racing thoughts, forgetfulness, disorganization, distraction, and pessimism.
- Behaviorally, stress may cause you to eat too much or too little, procrastinate, use alcohol or drugs, fidget, pace, or bite your nails.

The Color of Stress

Stress is associated with the color red:

Over time, chronic stress can lead to mental health problems, heart disease, obesity or other eating disorders, menstrual problems, sexual dysfunction, skin and hair issues, and digestive problems. The effects of stress are real and shouldn't be taken lightly.

My self-discovery journey started when stress became too much; feelings of overwhelm led to periods of shutdown. This lead-up to a tipping point is common for adult women and is my **'why' for creating Confetti Dreamers**. It makes me sad to think of all the women out there who are struggling because they are trying to live up to expectations that don't align with how their brains work. Life is hard, but it can also be so much more than survival. Life can be wonderfully marvelous, inspiring, and fulfilling.

You deserve to thrive.

Stress-related Terminology

Let's look at some terminology related to the effects of stress. *If you start to feel a weight on your shoulders as you read this section, have hope.* The next section, "Seeing the Light, Feeling the Hope," provides some coping strategies. (●●●)

Sensory Overload

Sensory overload occurs when you feel overwhelmed by all the information coming at you from your five senses. Removing yourself from an over-stimulating environment for a quiet reprieve can help. With each episode, your "reset" may not return you to your baseline; instead, your baseline can gradually inch toward your tipping point. This change in baseline is caused by an imbalance in your hormones, with high levels of cortisol being the culprit. While stress is part of life, if a person does not have tools to effectively regulate and reduce their stress, executive functioning becomes more difficult.

Executive Functioning

Executive functioning refers to how you manage tasks related to everyday life, including skills such as impulse control, flexible thinking, emotional control, working memory, self-monitoring, planning and prioritizing, task initiation, and organization (Karanzalis, 2019; ADDvantages Learning

Center, 2024). The quality of your executive functioning skills can decline when frequently stressed.

Meltdowns

Episodes of sensory overload and/or social stress can trigger a **meltdown**, which may involve yelling, aggression, self-harm, and repetitive behaviors. A person is not rational or reasonable during a meltdown. While you may have seen a person with Autism and high support needs experience a meltdown, the range of behaviors expressed during a meltdown can vary greatly. What is considered a meltdown for one person may look mild compared to someone with a more aggressive meltdown. Meltdowns of any kind are emotionally exhausting for the person experiencing them and can be for those providing support.

Shutdowns

Sometimes meltdowns turn into **shutdowns**. Sometimes shutdowns happen without a preceding meltdown. A shutdown is a retreat from the world—sometimes a physical retreat, but always a mental retreat. Typically, shutdowns are quiet retreats with little to no stimulus, allowing the person to reset from the stressful trigger(s). Some shutdowns are so subtle, they are unnoticeable to those nearby.

Burnout

Neurodivergent Insights with Dr. Neff provides numerous wonderful resources on Autism and ADHD. In one of her blog posts, Dr. Neff covers Autistic burnout symptoms. She references an article where the title itself defines Autistic burnout as "having all of your internal resources exhausted beyond measure and being left with no clean-up crew" (Raymaker et al., 2023).

When someone with Autism uses their highly developed survival strategy of masking to fit in and doesn't have the low-mid-high supports they need, they may experience Autistic burnout. The signs of burnout are like the signs of high stress, most specifically "pervasive fatigue, increased sensitivities, and loss of executive functioning skills" (Neff, 2024).

Triggers

Triggers can cause feelings of overwhelm, potentially leading to meltdowns and shutdowns. Sometimes triggers are like pet peeves, but on steroids.

Triggers are cues—accurate or not—that cause or worsen symptoms. Triggers elicit a reaction by moving the body into fight, flight, or freeze states.

Triggers related to sensory input and executive functioning can be external, like:

- too many demands or expectations
- an unexpected change in plans or routine
- sensory overload
- social overload

Or internal, such as:

- feelings of shame, guilt, inadequacy, or injustice
- feeling like you don't belong or feeling like you can't live authentically

Triggers can cause physical and emotional responses. Sometimes the "tipping" trigger that results in a meltdown or shutdown seems minuscule compared to other stressors. However, when a person's capacity for handling stress is full, one small droplet may be all it takes to cause an overflow.

Stress Bucket

A stress bucket is one analogy used to explain how stress can help or harm the state of your mental health (Brabban and Turkington, 2002).

- Envision a bucket that holds water/stress.
- The bucket has a spigot for releasing water/stress.
- Your bucket can only hold so much water/stress.
    - For some, their bucket may look like a fifty-gallon bucket, while others have a small pail.
    - The size of your bucket can fluctuate based on feelings of vulnerability, which may relate to feelings of (in)adequacy and (in)authenticity.

- When you are coping with the stressors of life, water flows from the faucet, giving you energy while decreasing the amount of water/stress in your bucket. This process is continuous and healthy.
- When the faucet is not working well (e.g., it's leaking, frozen, malfunctioning), water/stress fills the bucket, eventually overflowing.

I share the stress bucket analogy for several reasons:

- Stress isn't always a bad thing.
- When your bucket holds a manageable amount of stress, it can be invigorating.
- When someone feels overwhelmed, perhaps due to sensory overload, more water/stress comes in than goes out, and they may have more difficulty coping.
- Over time, this can lead to a full or overflowing bucket (i.e., meltdowns, shutdowns, burnouts).

If the stress bucket is a downer, there is hope. Truly. (●●●)

Spoons

"Spoons" is a metaphor for your energy level (Neff, 2023).

Allistics (non-Autistics or non-Autists) have a silverware drawer full of spoons, a seemingly endless amount of energy to tackle the day...the week...the month. You get the point.

Neurodivergent people may have a limited number of spoons for the day. This number can fluctuate—daily, weekly, monthly, based on your season of life, etc.

For example, if you have twelve spoons for the day, how would you decide which ones to use? What if the decision itself uses one of your spoons, leaving you with only eleven? What if the non-negotiables of routine life—job, school, children, significant other, meals, appointments, etc.—use an additional eight spoons? That leaves you with three spoons for the day. This is where the stress bucket may start to fill and get dangerously close to overflowing.

Think back to the diagram of co-occurring diagnoses. If an Autistic person also has ADHD, for example, they may experience bouts of depression or chronic fatigue from intense masking. This can translate to a continuous boom-or-bust cycle, where overexertion results in fatigue or burnout, necessitating rest. This cycle is quite frustrating, especially when compared to others with a drawer full of spoons, and even more so when feeling misunderstood and judged.

The next chapter shares some ideas for dealing with stress, so you can enjoy life more consistently.

Chapter 19

Seeing the Light, Feeling the Hope

The cool thing about color is that it can be used as a coping mechanism when learning to embrace your authentic self. When life feels overwhelming with literal or figurative clutter and noise, color can calm and soothe. Conversely, when you're feeling down, color can excite and energize.

Similar to people who experience seasonal depression due to a lack of sunlight during winter months, lighting can impact mood, especially for Autistic people. Fluorescent lighting can be evil (my interpretation), but so can dark, shadowy places when trying to see with clarity. As an Autist, I find myself adjusting the light around me all the time. Perhaps this sensitivity to light relates to my sensitivity to color.

I am keenly aware that color impacts my mood. I feel most satisfied when I see vibrant colors like fuchsia, cobalt blue, and marigold. As I sit and write, I am completely surrounded by lush greenery, a wall of warm bricks in earthy reds, yellows, and purples, pops of color from red and yellow Adirondack chairs, lavender phlox, and bright orange azaleas. It's practically heaven. However, when I enter a building washed entirely in white, gray, or beige, I hunger for spice. Thank goodness for vibrant art used to liven up such spaces.

What's interesting about Autism is the range of reactions to stimuli. It's common for people with Autism to experience seemingly contradictory reactions to stimuli. Hypersensitivity is common, resulting in feelings of overstimulation; however, hyposensitivity, which involves feelings of under-stimulation, requires 'loud' stimuli to feel comfortable. For example, an Autistic person can be highly overstimulated in crowds, yet prefer rocking out to heavy, loud music. This disparity can apply to color, too. For me, color can be overwhelming in shopping malls and museums, yet I immerse myself in color at home. Color can also be used to express yourself—from the colors you wear to how you decorate your personal space—and your personal brand.

What colors do you like to wear?

- Black and white
- Monochromatic colors, like shades of blues or grays
- Muted, earthy tones found in nature
- Blues, greens, or browns to enhance your eye color
- Busy, colorful patterns
- Bold, vibrant colors that pop
- It doesn't matter, as long as you're comfortable
- As you think about your brand and the role color plays in your life, you may find it can be used as a de-stressor, as well as a tool to unlock your true, authentic self.

Radiant Colors of Positivity

There's an alternative to feeling colors of stress, and that is feeling colors of glimmer. For example, this image stirs feelings of delight and optimism in me.[29] Personally, I prefer my headspace to exist within this burst of color. This section provides ideas on how you can achieve your own internal glimmer of color.

Spinning Into Control, quilt and photo by Ben Millett. Used with permission.

---

[29] https://benmillett.us

Glimmers

The term "glimmer" was introduced in 2018 by licensed clinical social worker, Deborah Dana (Neo, 2023; Blanchfield, 2023; Porges and Dana, 2018), and a viral TikTok video helped spread the word (Grosso, 2022).

Glimmers are cues of joy and safety to help regulate an overwhelmed nervous system. These cues help calm your nervous system by moving the body into the ventral vagal state. Glimmers can help you start to feel shimmers of your authentic color(s).

While it is important to understand what triggers stress, it is just as important to understand what makes your heart sing: rainbows, walking or running outside, a sincere and unexpected smile, basking in the sun, feeling the breeze in your hair, sparkles glistening on the water, cuddling with your fur baby, random acts of kindness, the perfect drink, soft clothes, and so on.

Want more than a micro glimmer? Be intentional about staying with the sensation for at least thirty seconds and feel the glow. When you proactively treat your nervous system to glimmers, these moments can ground you with feelings of connectedness. Being intentional about soaking up glimmers can help counterbalance our innate behavior of scanning for threats and danger.

Coping with Triggers

Recognizing your triggers and glimmers can help you find effective coping skills and de-stressing techniques. Here are some coping strategies for reducing the impact and strength of triggers (Ponte, 2022; UNC, 2024). **As you read, think about your color and vibrancy.**

Reflect. Think back to your past triggers: who, what, when, where, how, and why. Are there any patterns? Can this information help mitigate the risk of repeating the triggering scenario? What color do you feel when you're triggered?

- I reflect on e-v-e-r-y-t-h-i-n-g, so this should be easy for me, right? I wish. In some situations, yes. I reflect on any pain points

- in a project at work and come up with a plan to avoid that pain point in the future.
- When I look at my mental health over the past thirty-five years, there are clear cyclical patterns:
    - Start a job >> imposter syndrome >> over-produce to prove my value >> mask like crazy >> start feeling fatigue >> start getting triggered >> start fortune telling >> attack with black-and-white thinking >> get angry >> avoid conflict >> meltdown >> start looking for a new job. No, you are not the only one.
    - When I find myself in this pattern, I'm a hot mess of emotions and color.
    - I am aware of this recurring pattern, which is important. Therapy over the past four years and a deep dive into understanding my neurodivergence are helping.
- **What are some of your patterns?**

Make a plan of action. Others' behaviors may be triggering—gaslighting, passive-aggressiveness, intense negativity, narcissism, etc. Since you can't control other people, creating a plan for these triggers may involve setting boundaries for yourself. Think about what you can do to start minimizing your emotional reaction to triggers.

- For example, I have to limit the time I spend with someone who weighs me down and brings no positivity to the relationship. If I feel the onset of an overly negative emotional reaction, I walk away and take a breather. When I'm able to carry out my plan with intention, the vibrancy and combinations of my true colors start to grow. For me, this would be an analogous color scheme of magenta, purple, and blue.
- **Which tools or strategies have you tried? Which ones work well for you?**

Try problem-focused coping. Confront your stressor head-on or find a solution.

- My tolerance for noise has plummeted in adulthood. I've found earplugs helpful in spaces that are overstimulating. When I decide the reward of the loud environment is worth it, the earplugs help

dampen the noise. I can't wait to go to the AJR concert, but my earplugs will be in my pocket, ready to save the night.
- The smell of the laundry detergent aisle sends me over the edge. My family knows this and takes the scenic route with me to avoid sensory overload. I also feel angst when I go through a car wash because of the scent from the cleaner. Oh, and have you ever walked into a restaurant only to leave because of the cleaning solution they use on the tables and floors? There's an obvious sensory pattern for me with chemical smells, and I make conscious decisions to avoid those triggers to prevent headaches, itchy eyes, and other physical responses. In these situations, I feel an onslaught of spiky colors.
- **What could you try?**

Try emotion-focused coping. Use strategies, like meditation and mindfulness, to reduce your emotional reaction to a trigger.

- This has been a game-changer for me. After a strong nudge from my therapist, I participated in a seven-week meditation class where I learned how to meditate. The first class felt excruciatingly long. When I closed my eyes to meditate, I was distracted by my physical body. My legs would twitch, and I would hyperfocus on an itch I couldn't scratch. Each week, the instructor taught us a strategy and then guided us through practice; some strategies clicked more than others. Over time, I was able to completely relax in mindful meditation. To keep practicing with guidance, I signed up for the continuation class. Eventually, I found myself using it on my own, first as a tool when I was triggered, and now proactively to center myself. This transformation surprised me.
- Journaling has been another effective tool for me. My daughter Grace gave me *The Artist's Way: Morning Pages Journal* by Julia Cameron to spark my creative juices. It is a journal with specific guidelines: write in longhand, write daily, write in the morning, and write three pages. The author describes the journal as a word trail, a morning phone call to yourself, a tool to provoke and comfort, and/or a way to prioritize. Some days it was an easy ask; other days it was a chore—but the reward was worth it.
- When I start to feel a sense of Zen, my true colors radiate from both my heart and mind.

- **Have you tried meditation or journaling?**

Communicate. Often, a person may not realize they are triggering you. Try having a calm conversation with them to discuss your concern and possible solutions. Be open to compromise and working together. If they don't take you seriously and continue triggering you, you may have to set clear boundaries.

- Oh gosh. This one is the hardest one for me, partly because I act like a fortune teller. I run through various scenarios in my head before a conversation, *thinking* I know how the other person will respond. This results in an escalated situation before we even have the conversation. Ridiculous, right?
    - A friend suggested I frame a potential conversation in my mind as an informal, light-hearted conversation vs. an agenda. This minimizes the risk of me coming across too aggressively as I try to fulfill my agenda. Practice helps, but I have a long way to go.
    - I despise conflict, which is why I avoid hard conversations. The stress I feel leading up to difficult conversations makes me feel annoyed and fragile, like disparate swirls of fiery red and delicate ice. The after-color depends on how the conversation went. Sometimes the red deepens, but I'm delighted when it's a pink and yellow surprise of positivity.
- **How do you feel about having these types of conversations? How can you prepare for them?**

Look for trigger warnings. Trigger warnings alert you of potentially triggering content, like death or violence, so you can decide whether to skip the content.

- It seems like the use of trigger warnings is becoming more common. I hope this is an accurate perception.
- In the Facebook Group, Autistic Women+ Living Authentically, members are good about using trigger warnings, such as:
    - **TW: topic** (family issues) (meltdowns) (ableism) (pet loss) (addiction), etc.
- I find the list of trigger warnings shared by Autistic women+ interesting because, when seen as a list, they reflect some of the potential challenges for Autists—toxic relationships, effects

- of long-term masking, and maladaptive coping strategies. This underscores the importance of education and support.
- I like the idea of creating my own trigger warnings to protect myself from a flood of negative emotional and physical reactions. For example, while I like murder mysteries, startling sounds and violent imagery cause me to flinch and tighten my muscles. Why would I subject myself to this? I have become more selective in what I watch, read, or discuss as a tool to protect myself.
- If trigger warnings work well for you, consider asking others to provide trigger warnings about content they share.
  - My daughter Ellie did this proactively for me the other day, and I was so appreciative. She started to tell me something that involved an animal and death. She paused and asked if I was up for the conversation; I opted out because I was feeling too delicate. Instead, we talked about providing trigger warnings when conversing with others, something she uses with her friends. This made my heart happy, like a virtual hug in a rich rainbow of colors.
- **What trigger warnings would cause you to pause before exposing yourself to the content?**

Reality-check your thoughts. Ask yourself, "Is this reasonable?"

- Do a fact check. 1) What is undeniably accurate? 2) Do those facts support what you're thinking?
  - Rumors can be triggering, especially when disguised as truth. Instead of reacting, start by determining the facts. In the meantime, "wait to worry." This is my new favorite phrase.
- Reframe the thought. Turn a negative thought into a positive thought. This is not one of my strengths; however, I am lucky to have a friend who models this for me. I'm working on this, one baby step at a time.
  - My complaint: "My yard, which is on a double lot, is so much work. It sucks up all my time most of the year."
  - Her response: "You are so lucky to have a yard. Spending time in the dirt is the best medicine. And look at how beautiful it is."

- Check for proportionality. *Does the punishment match the crime? Does my reaction match the trigger?*
  - When a trigger is the last drop before a tipping point, the proportionality may be out of whack and hard to analyze without emotion. But, it's worth a try. Reaching the tipping point also underscores the importance of reflection and planning strategies.
- **Do you identify with over-the-top thoughts? It's okay to fact-check your brain; it needs it sometimes.**

Check for cognitive distortions. Your brain is wonderfully magnificent, wired to protect you. Yet, the brain can develop faulty connections, resulting in patterns of thinking that are simply not true. We inadvertently reinforce these irrational thoughts and beliefs over time until they become habits. Listening to these thoughts is not in our best interest.

While everyone experiences cognitive distortions to some degree, the potential impact spans the spectrum. Some people aren't fazed, while others really struggle. Yes, my hand is raised with those who struggle. To avoid getting stuck in a negative thought cycle, it is helpful to identify these types of thoughts and learn how to manage them. A qualified therapist can help you through this process, which can take time as your brain rewires and new patterns of thinking are practiced and learned.

Common Cognitive Distortions

Despite being a self-proclaimed (and diagnosed) distorted thinker, I try to reason with my brain. Maybe some of these tips will work for you, too.

- All-or-nothing thinking (aka black-and-white thinking or polarized thinking).
  - Key identifier: Everything is wonderful or awful.
  - Counter argument: We know better. Everything is on a range or spectrum—not just at the extremes, right?
- Overgeneralization
  - Key identifier: Always. Never.
  - Counter argument: Again, think about the spectrum. Instead of always or never, it's probably more like frequently, sometimes, occasionally, now and then, every so often, at times, seldom, or rarely.

- Mental filtering
    - Key identifier: Filter out the positives. Focus on negatives.
    - **Counter argument:** Why hover at one end of the spectrum when you can dip into the pot of gold throughout the journey?
- Discounting the positive
    - Key identifier: Acknowledge the positive, but reject it in lieu of embracing it.
    - **Counter argument:** You're really going to say, "No thank you" to the pot of gold? Throughout the lengthy process of writing this book, I tried to remind myself of this mantra: *Celebrate everything!* Positivity really can trick your brain into thinking more optimistically.
- Jumping to conclusions (mind reading)
    - Key identifier: Negative interpretations of what you think a person is thinking.
    - **Counter argument:** First, you can't read minds. Secondly, the range of possibilities is, you guessed it, likely on a spectrum. Consider resetting to a clean slate and approaching the conversation by assuming positive intent. *Phew! That's a tricky one.*
- Jumping to conclusions (fortune telling)
    - Key identifier: Make conclusions and predictions with no/little evidence **and** treat them as truth.
    - **Counter argument:** *See 'mind reading.'*
- Magnification (catastrophizing) or minimization
    - Key identifier: Worst-case scenario or exaggerating the meaning, importance, or likelihood of the negatives while minimizing the meaning, importance, or likelihood of the positives.
    - **Counter argument:** Sometimes I find it helpful to think about the worst-case scenario because it magnifies the absurdity of it.
- Emotional Reasoning
    - Key identifier: Trusting your emotions as fact.
    - **Counter argument:** Just because you feel something does not make it the truth. Do some fact-checking. It's good exercise for the brain.
- Should statements

- Key identifier: "I should," "I ought to," and "I must."
- **Counter argument:** Really? Who says? Okay, yes. Following the law is a good idea if you want to stay out of trouble; however, many "shoulds" are arbitrary guidelines with no enforcement.
- Labeling
  - Key identifier: An extreme form of overgeneralization that involves belittling name calling projected at yourself or someone else.
  - **Counter argument:** Seriously? Don't be so immature (talking to myself here). Oh, wait; calling myself immature is labeling. Let's not be so hard on ourselves. And again, check the facts, remove the emotion, and be reasonable with (and kind to) yourself.
- Personalization and blame
  - Key identifier: Taking everything personally and blaming yourself.
  - **Counter argument:** I ask myself, "Does everything revolve around you?" No. Sometimes plans change. That's it. You are not to blame.

I'm not sure why so many cognitive distortions apply to me, but I've spent hours on this in therapy.

Awareness is the first step to making changes. You, too, deserve to trust your brain, even if it requires a bit of guidance.

Practice self-care. You deserve to be acknowledged, cared for, and loved—**by you.**

Sometimes it's hard to know where to start.

Some ideas:

- Join a Facebook Group. I highly recommend Autistic Women+ Living Authentically.
- Look for opportunities to connect with others who have similar interests.
- Address your triggers.
- Talk to someone.

- - If you don't have a go-to person, look for a therapist. Consider online options if face-to-face feels too overwhelming.
  - Pets are great listeners, too.
- Look for ways to center yourself, such as meditation, journaling, nature walks, or yoga.
  - Maybe start with an online option. When you feel comfortable, branch out.
- Embrace your special interests. *Maybe you love color as much as I do.*

Self-care does wonders for my sense of contentment. I start to believe it when I tell myself, **"My favorite color is you!"**

Stimming

Stimming is another coping strategy. There are numerous examples of stimming—some stereotypically associated with Autism, some not: flapping hands, rocking, spinning or twirling, head banging, fidgeting, dancing, humming, whistling, swinging, tapping fingers, tapping ears or objects, playing with hair, playing with a necklace, counting things, skin picking, rubbing material, pacing, repeating words or phrases, picking or biting nails, shaking a leg or foot, blinking, staring blankly at objects or into space, chewing or biting lips, jumping, cracking knuckles, chewing pencils, snapping fingers, flicking fingers, and so on.

> What is stimming? Stimming is when someone moves their body repetitively and unconsciously to self-regulate (Mazefsky, Herrington, & Siegel, et al., 2013).

Stimming is not always socially acceptable, which is why these behaviors are often masked in public spaces. The good news is that this stigma is starting to lift, at least in baby steps. For example, fidget spinners exploded in popularity in 2017 as toys for helping people focus and reduce stress. Now, there's a plethora of sensory gadgets available, from stress balls, to tangles, silly putty, and Squishmallows. The market is hot with options.

Many forms of stimming are positive ways to cope, self-regulate, or focus, but can feel uncomfortable if masking is your superpower.

Kotowicz shares her personal evolution of stimming in her book, *What I Mean When I Say I'm Autistic*.

- **Bad:** I shouldn't let myself stim.
- **Good:** I should let myself stim when I feel like it.
- **Better:** I should remember, when I'm anxious or overwhelmed, that stimming is a strategy I can intentionally use to calm myself.
- **Best:** I should remember, when I'm about to enter a stressful situation, that stimming is a strategy I can use to prepare myself ahead of time.

Here are some stims to try (or continue doing):

- embrace the urge to flap your hands
- literally jump for joy if so inclined
- rub a soothing texture, like a soft blanket or pillow
- bounce your leg
- tap your foot
- hum
- sway side-to-side or back-and-forth
- rub your nose or touch your face
- twirl your hair
- practice typing with your fingers
- wrap yourself in a cocoon of soft blankets

Some stims can increase the risk of harm to oneself, such as head banging, skin picking, and biting oneself. These stims need to be monitored and possibly supplemented with less risky options (Kotowicz, 2022).

- For head banging, try deep pressure or swinging.
- For skin picking, try compression (like a weighted blanket), wear protection (gloves or hat), or rub soft, smooth textures.
- For biting oneself, try *chewelry*. It's a real thing! It's jewelry made for chewing.

Personally, when I'm able to let loose and stim, I feel authentically me. The color combination is reflective of my mood. If I'm feeling magenta, it becomes even more vibrant with contrasting confetti of chartreuse and periwinkle.

> From personal experience, it is helpful to be considerate of those around you, at least to some degree, because some types of stimming can be triggering for others. As much as we want others to accept us for who we are (our authentic selves), they want the same from us (for us to respect their authentic selves). This requires some give and take. If I feel the need to squeal at the top of my lungs and my husband has a headache, it is more respectful for me to go upstairs or outside.

Pacing

Think back to the five areas where skills and support needs can range from low, mid, to high. In the context of coping strategies, **pacing** is a framework to help you balance your energy levels and avoid a continuous boom-or-bust cycle.

Dr. Neff provides an overview and resources in *How to Use Pacing Systems* (Neff, 2023b), which include these ten steps to success:

1. Select a pacing system.
2. Do an inventory.
3. Monitor your energy.
4. Set clear goals.
5. Create a daily or weekly schedule.
6. Prioritize self-care.
7. Practice mindful check-ins.
8. Adjust and fine-tune.
9. Track and reflect.
10. Seek support.

Notice how some ideas from earlier are threaded into her list—self-care, mindfulness, self-reflection, and support. An easy button would simplify life, but through challenge comes growth. Be patient as you find what works best for you, and **enjoy the progression of color as your vibrancy starts to shine.**

Chapter 20

Should You Get a Diagnosis?

What if you relate to numerous items on the list of Autistic traits or the list of stress-related symptoms? Should you seek a diagnosis?

Deciding whether to pursue a diagnosis is very much a personal decision. The decision can be statically charged with raw emotions—especially if you have felt overwhelmed for much of your life and have been through other exhausting diagnostic processes. Before deciding whether to pursue a diagnosis, **consider your why.** Maybe it's curiosity. Or validation. Sometimes it's desperation.

Some women+ feel the nudge to explore (or reignite their exploration) after a series of stressful events negatively impacts their quality of life. They may start to wonder about the possibility of having a neurodivergent brain, including behaviors associated with Autism, and begin by **researching online** because it is safe and anonymous.

If it feels scary and intimidating, it may help if you frame the purpose of your research as a perpetual journey to understanding yourself.

When I started thinking of it as researching my brain and how it functions instead of "what is wrong with me," my fears diminished.

> Side note: This point of view has also made me more tolerant of other people's quirks. Their brains are unique, too. Perhaps they aren't intentionally being *[insert negative behavior here]*; rather, it's how their brain functions in an environment of *[insert factors here]*.

Self-Discovery Tools

I debated with myself for quite some time about what resources to share because I have neither the time nor the skills to vet them. It is not my intention to endorse or discount any resource; I'm simply sharing what helped me. If you join a Facebook group like Autistic Women+ Living Authentically, you can search for recommendations or make a post asking for tips.

> When it comes to researching your brain and pursuing a diagnosis, what's enough?
>
> Again, this is a personal decision.
>
> Any of these options may be enough for you:
>
> - reading about Autism in adult women
> - self-reflecting
> - self-assessing
> - self-identifying
> - self-diagnosing
> - seeking a formal diagnosis
> - coming to terms with the result of your formal diagnosis

Embrace Autism is a resource often shared for its user-friendly website and easy access to *Autism Tests for Adults*. As stated on the website, "online Autism tests can play an important role in your journey of self-discovery, and may inform your decision to pursue a formal diagnosis. For a professional diagnosis, please see a knowledgeable professional who is qualified to assess Autism, such as Dr. Engelbrecht ND RP" (Embrace Autism, 2024).

The Embrace Autism website includes *Autism Tests for Adults*, which includes multiple tests, with basic information about the test, including the number of questions and a short description. At the time this was written, the tests included these:

- Short Autism Spectrum Quotient (AQ-10)
- AQ | Autism Spectrum Quotient
- EQ | Empathy Quotient
- SQ | Systemizing Quotient-Revised
- RAADS-R | Ritvo Autism Asperger Diagnostic Scale-Revised
- Aspie Quiz
- CAT-Q | Camouflaging Autistic Traits Questionnaire
- RBQ-2A | Repetitive Behaviours Questionnaire
- ASRS-5 | Adult ADHD Self-Report Scale for DSM-5

A second section, *Other Tests for Adults*, are designed to "offer insight into Autism and related aspects (empathy, camouflaging, executive skills, etc.) and co-occurring conditions (alexithymia, ADHD, etc.)" Many of these weren't available when I did my self-assessment, which shows how this space is ever-evolving.

- Online Alexithymia Questionnaire
- TAS | Toronto Alexithymia Scale
- TEQ | Toronto Empathy Questionnaire
- EDA-QA | Extreme Demand Avoidance Questionnaire
- ASRS v1.1 | ADHD Self-Report Scale v1.1
- ASRS-5 | ADHD Self-Report Scale for DSM-5
- VIA | Inventory of Strengths
- Big 5 | The Big Five Inventory-A
- VASQ | Vulnerable Attachment Style Questionnaire
- LSAS | The Liebowitz Social Anxiety Scale
- ESQ | Executive Skills Questionnaire

- ESQ-R | Executive Skills Questionnaire: Revised
- Y-BOCS | Yale-Brown Obsessive-Compulsive Scale
- RMET | Reading the Mind in the Eyes test: Revised
- CRT | Cognitive Reflection Tool

For me, my results from the self-assessments reinforced the "aha" feeling from joining the Facebook group, but I needed time to process the information. I didn't get caught up in the scores or breakdowns; the validation was enough. The self-diagnosis felt right, but imposter syndrome left me questioning.

Getting a Diagnosis

Why get a diagnosis?

The long-term effects of *having* ASD and *not* knowing it are real. So very real.

From the emotional toll of not fitting in and our misunderstood behaviors (meltdowns, shutdowns, and burnouts), our social lives and work lives can be noticeably and negatively impacted. If working becomes too much, economic issues are added to the mix, further complicating an already difficult situation. If getting a diagnosis can help mitigate those risks, perhaps it is worth it. It was for me.

Getting a diagnosis can help address some of these challenges and improve quality of life (Bargiela & Steward, 2016). How so?

Getting a diagnosis can help:

- recognize how your brain works (it's a gift, not a curse)
- acknowledge and validate your challenges
- identify your needs and, more importantly, potential solutions
- obtain a framework for strategizing
- increase access to services, like accommodations
- influence others' perceptions of your needs, with hope of increasing compassion and decreasing judgment
- identify and reduce self-critical thoughts and behaviors, with a goal to develop a positive, authentic sense of self

Diagnostic Resources

What options are available for getting a diagnosis?

The primary options are self-diagnosis and clinical diagnosis. I've included self-realization/self-identification as another alternative.

Self-diagnosis: This is when you research Autism and identify with many of the symptoms and presentations. This can include taking Autism tests for adults and using the interpreted results to determine you are Autistic. With this option, you are not evaluated by a provider.

Self-realization/self-identification: If you feel conflicted with the term "diagnosis," you might consider switching semantics. Perhaps you relate to this statement by Devon Price (2019): "You have a self-realization of Autism and you self-identify as Autistic."

Price shares a quote that may explain why joining the Facebook group was so impactful to me: **"Everything useful that I've learned about Autism, I have learned from Autistic people."**

Clinical diagnosis: This is when you work with a healthcare provider—a psychologist, psychiatrist, neuropsychologist—who is trained in assessing Autism in adults. A clinical diagnosis is also called a formal diagnosis or official diagnosis.

The process is thorough and time-consuming because the evaluator collects information about your history (from you, as well as from a parent, family member, or caregiver), conducts a series of tasks and observations, gives structured interviews to assess various criteria, and then synthesizes all the information into a report (Marschall, 2022).

If you go this route, consider looking for a "Neurodiversity-Affirming" organization, like ones on this list:

- Autistic Self Advocacy Network
- Embrace Autism
- Inclusive Therapists

- NeuroClastic
- Therapist Neurodiversity Collective

> What's up with a self-diagnosis?
>
> There is some controversy over the validity of self-diagnosis of Autism Spectrum Disorder. **But guess what? The flip side is also true.** There is controversy surrounding the process for clinically diagnosing ASD, too.
>
> So, what's the deal?
>
> By age eighteen, 80% of Autistic females remain undiagnosed (UCLA Health, 2023). **Wow!** But what does that mean?
>
> That's a loaded question with a complex answer.

Many Autistic women+ remain undiagnosed because of equity issues—disparities in health insurance and access to providers, as well as biased assessments.

Other factors:

- Professionals have little to no training in their postgraduate study on non-stereotypical presentations of Autism. If this applies, they really need to seek professional development in this area.
- Many professionals' assumptions about Autism presentation and the assessment measures they use, are based on research from samples that are primarily white, cismale, and children.
- There's limited research on adults. Emerging research is primarily qualitative and considered less robust because psychologists and doctors have a preference for large scale studies that find patterns across large samples for generalizable findings.
    - Note: Qualitative research is highly valid for minority populations, as well as reflective and honoring of the diversity of Autistic presentations.

Bottom line: If we look at the pros and cons of each, it's apparent—getting an Autism diagnosis can be complicated (and is a very personal decision).

Pros of Self-Diagnosis / Self-Identification:

- This is a no-cost option.
- No one knows you better than you.
- Only you can validate this statement: "This is who I truly am; my life now makes sense."
- If there's room for error either way, at least it's coming from the heart.
- People who suspect they have Autism spend hours, days, weeks, months, even years of research. Whereas Neurotypical folks don't.
- If you're self-diagnosed and you implement strategies to meet your needs and notice a drastic improvement, how marvelous!

Cons of Self-Diagnosis and Self-Identification:

- Some people won't take you seriously; they assume the clinical process is superior.
- You may not qualify for accommodations without a clinical diagnosis.

Pros of Clinical Diagnosis:

- This is considered acceptable "proof" by some people and for some circumstances.
- An official diagnosis can help you get academic or workplace accommodations.
- As more women get diagnosed, it will help inform research (which is desperately needed), as well as influence/shift the narrative away from a negative stigma.

Cons of Clinical Diagnosis:

- Misdiagnosis is common.
    - Think of all those co-occurring diagnoses; they often come before an ASD diagnosis.

- False negatives: "You are **not** Autistic."
  - This is devastating if you thought the "experts" were going to say "you are Autistic," but instead, they disagree.
  - Sadly, some underqualified providers try to convince people they are not Autistic despite the overwhelming evidence. "How can you be Autistic? You can hold a conversation and make eye contact. You don't even look Autistic." Seriously? Seriously.
- The costs are unrealistic.
  - Some health insurance plans don't cover an Autism evaluation for adults.
  - In the United States, out-of-pocket costs are typically $800-$5,000.
- Long waitlists are common.
  - After finding most providers in my area had closed their waitlists, I ended up waiting about a year to start the evaluation process.
  - I've heard of four-year waitlists (!) in some countries.
- The assessments are biased.
  - The tests to diagnose Autism were created by neurotypicals/allistics, initially for boys.
  - Tests still favor cisgender boys or men.
  - Masking presents itself in different ways in adults, women, people of color, transgender people, and poor people (Price, 2019).
- Lack of access to qualified providers.
  - "Qualified providers" include more than licensure. It also means the provider understands what masking is and how ASD presents in women+.
- The diagnosis may go on a permanent medical record, which could potentially lead to stigma and discrimination (e.g., employment bias, custody challenges, adoption obstacles, immigration issues).

What to Expect When You're Expecting a Formal Diagnosis

Oh, gosh. Reactions to clinical evaluations and results run the gamut—a spectrum. Often, the whole process is an emotional experience, particularly the grand finale. I recommend planning some recovery time on days scheduled for assessment and post-assessment.

What you might feel when you get your diagnosis:

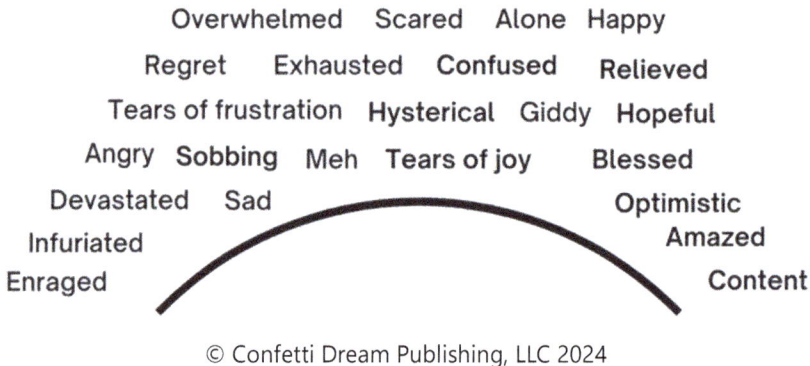

© Confetti Dream Publishing, LLC 2024

When formally diagnosed with Autistic Spectrum Disorder (ASD), the level of support is part of the diagnosis.

The number relates to the level of support needed:

- ASD-1 = Level 1 = Requiring some support
- ASD-2 = Level 2 = Requiring substantial support
- ASD-3 = Level 3 = Requiring very substantial support

What Next?

When you realize you are Autistic, it will take time to process. Days, weeks, months, or even years.

This is when you might find it particularly helpful to search for posts where others share their experience, or perhaps post about your journey.

Some tips for being kind to yourself during the process:

- It is not a death sentence. Far from it.
- Now you can work on accepting your true self.
- Be patient with any bouts of imposter syndrome.
- Connect to the Autistic Community (e.g., peer support groups, Facebook support groups).
- If your therapist doesn't support the diagnosis, it's worth finding someone who does.
- Work with a therapist to help undo past trauma and embrace your authentic self with kindness and compassion.
- Lean into your curiosity.
- Find your passion(s).
- Let yourself experience profound joy.

Accommodations

In the United States, **Section 504** of the **Rehabilitation Act of 1973** is a national law that protects qualified individuals from discrimination based on their disability. This law applies to any program or activity receiving funds from the U.S. Department of Education, including public school districts, institutions of higher education, and other state and local education agencies. Accommodations are critical for compliance.

> What are accommodations?
>
> Accommodations are alterations made to environment, curriculum format, or equipment that allows an individual with a disability to gain access to content and/or complete assigned tasks (Washington.edu, 2022).

For example, individualized education plans (IEPs) are used in grades K-12 in the United States to identify needs and describe accommodations to help ensure needs are being met for all students. In higher education, students can request accommodations, typically through the Disability Services office, as tools to help set them up for success.

Though Autism Spectrum Disorder (ASD) can be a hidden disability, meaning it's not outwardly apparent, the law still applies.

Academic accommodations for ASD may include things like:

- in-class notetakers
- course materials available in alternative formats (written, audio, video)
- alternative test-taking location with less sensory overload
- some flexibility with attendance
- a designated space in the dorm to recover from sensory overload

Title III, a law like Section 504, applies to businesses open to the public.

Workplace accommodations for ASD may include:

- a flexible work schedule
- alternative formats (written or verbal)
- adjusted lighting in the area from fluorescent to warm lighting
- a fragrance-free zone

Likely Pushback

You can't win if you are trying to please everyone. *Something I'm reminding myself of here, too.*

If you self-diagnose or self-identify, you may get pushback from non-Autistics (allistics) and possibly even from clinically diagnosed Autistics. On the other hand, some will actively oppose or question a formal diagnosis, if you go that route.

Don't ever feel obligated to apologize for **how you choose to learn about your brain.**

- If you have a self-realization of Autism, yay for you!
- If you self-identify, yay for you!
- If you self-diagnosis, yay for you!
- If you self-identify/diagnose and want to get a clinical diagnosis, yay for you!
- If you get a clinical diagnosis, yay for you!

And by the way, it's your prerogative if you want to let someone know you're on a waitlist. If we treat the formal diagnosis as required (you'll get it when you can get in), it perpetuates the underlying message that a clinical diagnosis is superior. (It's not.)

When Sharing: I'm Autistic

Think back to cognitive distortions and the one about mind reading. Since I 'think' I'm a gifted mind reader, sometimes I assume others are, too.

When on a self-discovery journey with Autism, you will most likely take time to mull it over, process it, and turn it inside out and upside down. It's easy to forget that others haven't been on the same journey. When they react to your news, their reactions may not live up to your expectations. It may sound flat, rude, ignorant, condescending, or questioning—all sorts of negative things. However, since we can't read minds, their hearts or intentions may come from a place of **un**knowing. Patience is important.

You may hear things like:

- I wondered.
- You can't be. You don't look Autistic.
- Isn't everyone a little bit Autistic?
- How is that possible? You're in your [20s/30s/40s/50s/60s/70s/80s/90s].
- It seems like everyone I know is Autistic.
- How do you know?

Here are some responses or phrases you might find helpful when figuring out how to respond to others:

- It has been so helpful to learn how my brain works.
- There's a lot of misinformation out there. By sharing my diagnosis, I'm speaking up against outdated stereotypes.
- What an odd thing to say out loud.
- Autism is a spectrum and can look different every day.
- I'm learning not to hide the real me. I love my Autistic traits!
- I'm proud to be Autistic. Knowing more about myself is so freeing.

- The number of people diagnosed with Autism **is** increasing, so there's a good chance you do know many Autistic people.
- I've learned so much on my journey. I'd love to share more if you're interested.
- Autism is misunderstood by many, yes, but Autism is not a bad thing.
- In my (our) circle, I'm (we're) surrounded by so many Autistic people. Isn't it great?
- Well, as women, we sure are good at masking, so it's hard to know for sure. As more women are diagnosed, more research can be done, which will help us better understand it.
- Not everyone is born Autistic or has traits that impact their everyday functioning.
- The good news is there are online tests to help explore your traits. I'm happy to share the website with you.
- It might seem like we're all a bit Autistic, but most people have just a few of the traits, like sensory issues or social anxiety. It's a special blend to be Autistic.
- Interesting fact. Evidence from twin and family studies estimates between 80-90% heritability of Autism. No wonder so many of us in our family have traits (Sandin et al., 2017).
- We all may have some Autistic traits, but not everyone goes down the rabbit hole to uncover all there is to know about it.
- A friend recently told me about being a Delilaa–**D**iagnosed **E**xtremely **L**ate **I**n **L**ife **A**s **A**utistic (D-E-L-I-L-A-A) (Gage, 2024). It's never too late to learn about yourself and embrace it.

For more ideas, Rebecca Burgess from The Art of Autism, created a comic strip where Archie explains different areas of the spectrum and how to respond to comments about being a little Autistic (Burgess, 2022). *I love it!*

Adapting to the New You: Plan or Wing It

I like to plan, but…

- Sometimes I don't plan, and the result is surprising *(either in a good way or bad way).*

- Sometimes the *plan* exceeds the *implementation*. Well, that didn't go as planned. That's okay.

I did not plan my journey into neurodiversity and Autism. In fact, it caught me by surprise.

Here's how my journey unfolded:

- I hit burnout. It was big, bad, and ugly. *Well, that's how it felt.*
- I joined the Facebook Group Autistic Women+ Living Authentically.
    - I followed the group rules and defined my own guidelines for interacting with the group.
    - I scoured the posts.
    - I engaged with the content with emojis and comments.
    - Occasionally, I posted a question or comment.
    - I ignored posts with certain types of trigger warnings (TW).
    - I reflected on how it felt to be part of the group. It was incredibly validating. I felt included, like I belonged. I had found my tribe.
- I explored and researched to learn more.
    - I completed some online assessments.
    - I looked into assessment options in my area.
    - I looked up the pros/cons of getting a diagnosis.
- I reflected on what works for me and what doesn't.
    - I acknowledged what stimuli or environments trigger me, from mild discomfort to fix-it-now!
    - I also acknowledged what relaxes and calms me. I tried many coping strategies and found some go-to options.
- I planned ways to make situations work better for me.
    - Layered clothing, water bottle, snacks, noise-canceling earbuds/headset, mini breaks away from the noise, fidget toys, etc.
- I considered whether it would be helpful to request and document my accommodation needs at work.
- With trepidation, I got on a waitlist to be assessed.
    - I was careful to find someone who was trained in the presentation of Autism in women. Still, I felt fear, doubt, excitement, confidence, apprehension, anxiety, and peace—simultaneously.

- I was diagnosed with Autism Spectrum Disorder, Level 1.
    - Thank goodness, because I was nearly finished writing this book. Seriously, this is true. My self-discovery journey provided the clarity I needed to fuel this book.
- I asked myself:
    - What color are you?
    - How vibrant is your color?
    - Does your color and vibrancy tend to stay the same or vary?
    - Do these colors and vibrancy reflect your authentic self?

Regardless of whether you decide to plan or wing it, there will be surprises along the way. Be kind to yourself. *And be kind to others.* Getting to know a "new you" requires patience and perseverance.

The next chapter circles back to Maslow's Hierarchy of Needs and takes a close look at what living authentically might look like when you embrace your true colors.

Chapter 21

Maslow's Hierarchy of Needs in Color

On my journey to learn more about how my brain works (and not what's wrong with it), I kept thinking about Maslow's Hierarchy of Needs. Although it's not my area of expertise, I understand the basic premise.[30] It is a motivational theory with five levels of needs, starting with basic survival as the foundation. As a person's needs are met, they can move up to the next level of the hierarchy.

---

[30] Check out this explanation (Mcleod, 2024): https://www.simplypsychology.org/maslow.html

© Plateresca 2017

When you embrace your authentic self, your true colors become clearer and more vibrant as you move up the hierarchy. This chapter describes how my journey of self-discovery progressed and presented itself in shades of blue. Because everyone's color journey is as unique as their fingerprint, this chapter supplements my personal journey with other examples.

Physiological Needs

Maslow refers to this first level as **physiological needs** because it relates to what our bodies need for **survival**: air, water, food, sleep, shelter, and clothing. Using blue for illustration purposes, my base layer is a grayish blue.

As a person's needs are met, they are motivated to pursue higher levels. If you are in a constant state of fight-or-flight, survival is your top priority. It is difficult to move up the pyramid if you constantly hover near your tipping point or experience an Autistic burnout. This is why it is important to find ways to stabilize and care for your nervous system and cultivate a life that nurtures your wonderfully wired brain.

Side note: If you constantly mask to fit in, you become a chameleon. While chameleons are amazing creatures with a miraculous ability to blend into their surroundings, being a human chameleon means you are not being authentically you, which can become utterly exhausting. Autistic women+ often have masking superpowers, which sounds awesome. Until it isn't. Protecting yourself from being noticed for not fitting in requires constant masking, which can result in debilitating mental health issues and chronic health conditions.

Safety Needs

When your physiological needs are met—that is, you have stable shelter, clothing, food, and a (fairly) routine sleep cycle—the next level is your **safety needs**. This is when you can become more established and independent. Often, this translates to securing a job, housing, healthcare, and other "adult" expectations. This layer can be challenging for some Autistic women+, depending on their presentation of low, mid, or high skills and support needs. In my example, the "safety needs" layer would be a pastel blue.

For example, sensory overload and unpredictable social interactions can make full-time employment difficult. The reality of this layer is—you guessed it—a spectrum. Because income can impact other areas such as housing, security, health, and resources, it can be an important requirement. For adults with Autism and co-occurring diagnoses like ADHD, employment can be challenging.

Employment can take a variety of forms:

- working part-time with a job coach
- working part-time independently
- working full-time
- working multiple jobs
- working overtime

A real challenge in today's world is when income is not enough to meet basic monthly needs. This financial deficit forces hard decisions:

- Decreasing your work hours for your mental health means less income.
- Increasing your work hours to make ends meet may increase emotional stress.
- Penny pinching and living paycheck to paycheck can be stressful.
- Living beyond your means causes other problems.

Decisions related to fulfilling your safety needs can be overwhelming. If this area is challenging for you, try searching the area where you live for employment-related resources. Certain types of jobs and accommodations can help set you up for success.

Love and Belonging

Let's consider the next layer of Maslow's hierarchy: **love and belonging**. This layer includes friendship, intimacy, family, and a sense of connection. I envision this layer of "love and belonging" as a primary 'blue' crayon, a color I can count on.

According to Maslow, needs are typically met in one layer before moving to the next; however, this is not a clear-cut rule. For example, an adult can feel love and belonging even if they don't have a stable job. If we look at Maslow's intention, it is more realistic to feel a sense of belonging and love if you have strategies for meeting your basic physiological and safety needs.

But let's face it, interpersonal relationships can be hard. This can be especially true for Autistic women+. Stories of bullying, aggression, gaslighting, and ghosting are not uncommon; however, the reasons why these negative experiences happen are complex, layered, and tricky to address. If you think back to the "Challenges" listed in the table of Autistic traits, some traits—like not remembering faces, not being able to name emotions, or rigid thinking—can make it more difficult to navigate friendships.

When I conducted research for my master's capstone, I received permission to get feedback from the Facebook group for Autistic women+. Many of the participants expressed sincere gratitude for the group because they felt validated and connected. They felt a true sense of belonging; they had found their tribe. In a social world that may not always be prepared for us, social media can be a safer way to fulfill our needs, especially when the space is well moderated to foster safety.

For me, this quote by diversity and inclusion expert Verna Myers makes the "sense of belonging" come alive.

Esteem

The next layer of Maslow's hierarchy is **esteem**, which amplifies your sense of connection, resulting in feelings of respect, positive self-esteem, strength, and freedom. I became a more vibrant blue—let's say cerulean—after researching and self-identifying as Autistic. I attribute this enthusiasm to the shift in how I now frame my thinking. It's no longer, "What's wrong with me?" It's simply, "How does my brain process information?" This new outlook has been liberating. I now feel an amazing sense of belonging, peace, and purpose that was missing.

Self-Actualization

Lastly, the top of the hierarchy is **self-actualization**, the desire to become the most you can be. It doesn't mean you're in a constant state of euphoria; rather, it is a continuous growth process of 'becoming' (Mcleod, 2024). This is where you are authentically YOU! Envision a GIF with a parade of pulsating hearts, flying unicorns, glitter, and sparkles. For me, some days this is cobalt blue glass. Other days, it is a crystal ball casting rainbows of color across the room. Sometimes, it is a rainbow of the most vibrant colors. The great news: it can be whatever you want it to be! Color *is* life, a basic human need.

My sincere hope is for you to reach periods of self-actualization.

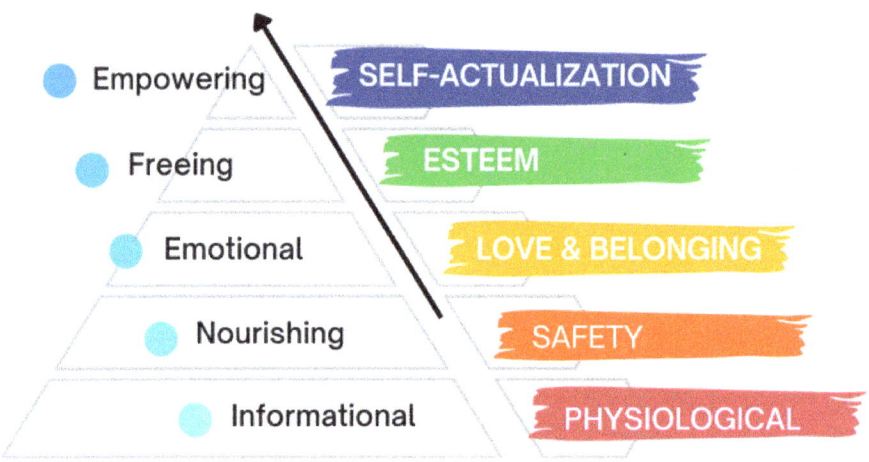

© Confetti Dream Publishing, LLC 2024

What Are Your True Colors?

This doesn't have to be a static answer, but it can be.

It is not my intention or recommendation to start using Maslow's Hierarchy all the time for determining your authentic color(s). That sounds hard and exhausting.

Instead, I provided it as a framework to explain the importance of taking care of yourself (meeting your needs) so you can live your best life as authentically as possible. Because of my obsession with color, I associated stages of contentment with key points from Part One of this book.

Answering these questions might help you identify your true colors:

- Which colors speak to you the most? Which ones are yummy?
- Which colors evoke negative feelings?
- How do your favorite colors vary based on your mood?
- Have your favorite colors changed with the changing seasons of life?
- Do you feel more vibrant on a really good day?
- Do you feel consistently comfortable with certain colors?
- Does your aura match what you're experiencing in life?
- What color formulas soothe you?
- What colors or color combinations trigger you?

> When someone says, "You have a wonderful aura about you," what does that mean? It means the person radiates positivity.
>
> Auras are colors that connect the dots between a person, their energy, and their color. An aura photograph literally captures a person's electromagnetic energy in the moment by using a special Polaroid camera (Aura Cam 6000) with hand sensors to gather the energy of the subject, which is then translated to a color on the visible light spectrum (Lonsdale, 2021).

I share this for those who know their aura colors, because they may be your true colors. While aura colors are typically steady, they can change if your body is reacting to a life event. I would be curious to see if a person's aura photographs change from the "before" picture of a highly stressed person who masks all the time, to the "after" picture of the same person who has embraced a life of authenticity.

As you start to identify your true colors, you can use this awareness to help you express your authentic self—perhaps by the colors you wear or use in your surrounding environment. More importantly, you can live authentically through color by cultivating a life that nurtures your uniquely and wonderfully wired brain.

Side Note: It's No Accident

Everything happens for a reason.

When I look back on my life and reflect on all the events (big and small), there is always a forward purpose or connection. I feel pure joy when seemingly unrelated events connect, and they are everywhere. All the time.

There are many ways people explain these connections:

- It's a God-thing.
- The stars aligned.
- It's synchronicity.
- It relates to your astrological sign.
- It's a fluke.

Regardless of your explanation, I hope this book was informative and provided kernels of inspiration. I hope it ended up in your hands when you needed it most.

A Serendipitous Moment in My Journey...

I happened upon the perfect book.

The Proudest Color! by Modir, Kashou, & Mikai (2021) is a delightful book about Zahra's experience seeing vivid colors and embracing her rich brown skin. When I read the first sentence, I felt as if they wrote the book to accompany mine: "I am like a box of crayons—bright and colorful. I see and feel in color."

It sounds like Zahra is a confetti dreamer.

Epilogue

My color journey has been full of so many delightful surprises.

If I were to map it out, it would look like a crazy quilt, complete with fabric and embellishments from along the way. It would include an analogous color scheme of blues, greens, and purples with surprising flecks of magenta and lime green. It would combine areas of dark quiet with bursts of sequins, glass beads, and bits of frenetic chaos. The edges would be delightfully imperfect—a combination of floundered attempts at expert seams, uneven hand stitches, and frayed raw edges.

It would be the perfect representation of me.

Your Invitation

I invite you to embrace your authentic self.

Regardless of whether you have or suspect a diagnosis in the realm of neurodivergence or Autism, everyone deserves to experience this color-rich world with utter abandon.

How does one go from survival to living authentically in color?

Become a confetti dreamer. Be authentically you. The colorful you, with your quirks, stims, and passion.

Confetti Dreamer

Color
Outside
Normalcy.
Forever
Embrace
Talents.
Tickle
Inspiration.

Do
Real.
Evolve
Authentically.
Marvel
Enthusiastically.
Repeat.

© Confetti Dream Publishing, LLC

Learn how to adapt to the new you!

Get your free guide today: ConfettiDreamers.com/NewYou

Live authentically through color by embracing the confetti dreamer in you.

Books About Color

When I started my journey, I checked out so many books from the library. In the grand scheme of books on color, this list represents a small fraction of what you can find:

- Try color-mixing experiments to help you self-discover the truths and mysteries of color.
    - Solomon, L. (2019). *A Field Guide to Color: A Watercolor Workbook* (First Edition). Roost Books.
- Apply color theory to mix, match, complement, harmonize, and surprise.
    - Fraser, T., & Banks, A. (2004). *Designer's Color Manual: The Complete Guide to Color Theory and Application.* Chronicle Books.
    - Sidaway, I. (2002). *Color Mixing Bible.* Watson-Guptill Publications.
- Successfully work with paint types—watercolor, oils, acrylics.
    - Sidaway, I. (2002). *Color Mixing Bible.* Watson-Guptill Publications.
    - Canal, M. F., Brunel, M., & Cortabarria, B. (2013). *The Practical Handbook of Color for Artists.* Barron's.
- Harvest pigments from nature for pure color.
    - St. Clair, K. (2017). *The Secret Lives of Color.* Penguin Books.
    - Kupferschmidt, K. (2021). *Blue: In Search of Nature's Rarest Color.* The Experiment.

- Use neighborly terms to remember the color wheel—next-door neighbors (analogous colors), the family across the road (complementary colors), and the family reunion (multicolored).
    - McCauley, I., & Pederson, S. (2007). *Color for the Terrified Quilter: Plain Talk, Simple Lessons, 11 Projects.* That Patchwork Place.
- Choose a color palette to create spaces that are [(fill in the blank)].
    - Spaces that are [harmonious] [calming] [energizing] [welcoming] [mysterious] [the list goes on…]
    - I love this one: Levin, Susan (2008). ColorSense: Creative Color Combinations for Crafts. Sixth & Spring Books.
    - Calderon, A. V. (2020). *Color Harmony for Artists: How to Transform Inspiration into Beautiful Watercolor Palettes and Paintings*. Quarry Books.
- Use plant dyes as a healthy alternative for coloring materials to your reduce carbon footprint and provide a less toxic option to synthetic coloring processes
    - Duerr, S. (2020). *Natural Palettes: Inspiration from Plant-based Color* (First edition). Princeton Architectural Press.
- Arrange our world into rainbows of color.
    - Seriously, check this out: Ream, J. S. (2017). *Encyclopedia of Rainbows: Our World Organized by Color.* Chronicle Books LLC.
- Adopt trendy colors…only to have them fade away and morph into iconic memories.
    - Adams, S. (2017). *Color Design Workbook: A Real-world Guide to Using Color in Graphic Design.* Quarto Pub Group USA.
- Use color in [(fill in the blank)] to create [(fill in the blank)].
    - Baekgaard, B. B. (2017). A Colorful Way of Living. St. Martin's Press.
    - Browning, M. (2013). *Time to Tangle with Colors.* Fox Chapel.
    - Deeb, M. (2008). *The Beader's Color Palette: 20 creative projects, 220 Inspired Combinations for Beaded and Gemstone Jewelry.* Watson-Guptill.

References for Part One | Color

Adams, S. (2017). *Color Design Workbook: A Real-world Guide to Using Color in Graphic Design.* Quarto Pub Group USA.

Clamp, M. (2023, November 3). *What Colors Make Brown?* Michele Clamp Art. https://micheleclamp.com/what-colors-make-brown/

Crayola. (n.d.). *Colors of the World. Crayola.com.* https://www.crayola.com/product-feature/colors-of-the-world

Dewey, M. (2019, May 13). *Artist's White Paint: What You Need to Know (Part One).* YouTube. https://www.youtube.com/watch?v=lCROd-22EMg

Dewey, M. (2017, May 15). *How to Mix Dark Color (Without Using Black Paint).* YouTube. https://www.youtube.com/watch?v=rMAJwTHApWQ

Eckstut, J. (2013). *The Secret Language of Color: Science, Nature, History, Culture, Beauty of Red, Orange, Yellow, Green, Blue & Violet.* Black Dog & Leventhal Pub.

Ellis, M. (2022, November 11). *RGB VS CMYK: What's the Difference?: Vistaprint US. Vistaprint Ideas and Advice US.* https://www.vistaprint.com/hub/correct-file-formats-rgb-and-cmyk

Empowered By Color. (n.d.) *Color Psychology Will Empower your Life*. https://www.empower-yourself-with-color-psychology.com/

EnChroma. (n.d.). *Enchroma® Color Blind Glasses: Color Blind Eyewear*. EnChroma. https://enchroma.com/

Fussell, M., & Hurst, A. (2019, September 3). *Color Theory and Mixing with Artists Matt Fussell and Ashley Hurst*. YouTube. https://www.youtube.com/watch?v=tmMcRjE98II&t=1484s

Gareth, David. (2016, April 14). *"Proximity" Design Principle of Graphic Design EP13/45 [Beginners Guide to Graphic Design]*. YouTube. https://www.youtube.com/watch?v=xUdqSiI_G8Y

Greenfield, L. (2020, July 14). *Acrylic Color Mixing: Skin Tones of all Shades*. YouTube. https://www.youtube.com/watch?v=zYys8v7qXio

Heath, K. (2022, June 29). *All About the Color Wheel | Mix any Color*. YouTube. https://www.youtube.com/watch?v=LCDW_V9P-U4

Konstantinovsky, M., & Bowie, D. (2023, September 13). *Primary Colors Are Red, Yellow and Blue, Right? Not Exactly*. HowStuffWorks Science. https://science.howstuffworks.com/primary-colors.htm

Levin, Susan (2008). *ColorSense: Creative Color Combinations for Crafts*. Sixth & Spring Books.

Lonsdale, C. (2021). *Radiant Human: Discover the Connection Between Color, Identity, and Energy*. Harper Design, an Imprint of HarperCollins Publishers.

Malik, R. (n.d.). *How to Use a Triadic Color Scheme to Make Your Designs Stand Out*. Leading Global UI UX Design Agency. Onething Design Studio. https://www.onething.design/blogs/triadic-color-scheme/

McIntyre, C. (2021, January 23). *Why Is Mixing Gray so Important for Painters? Celebrating Color*. https://www.celebratingcolor.com/mixing-gray/

Modir, S., Kashou, J., & Mikai, M. (2021). *The Proudest Color!* (First Edition). Familius LLC.

Nicoguaro (2016). *Ishihara Plate No. 1 (Number 12). Used for the en:Ishihara Test of Color Blindness.* Wikimedia Commons. Retrieved March 29, 2024. https://commons.wikimedia.org/w/index.php?curid=47050887

Pamela's Passion for Pencils. (2021, January 25). *How to Color Skin with Crayola 'Colors of the World' Colored Pencils | Adult Coloring for Beginners.* YouTube. https://www.youtube.com/watch?v=Y_ULhVT3bq0

Sarah Renae Clark. (2020c). *Color Theory Basics: Use the Color Wheel and Color Harmonies to Choose Colors That Work Well Together.* YouTube. Retrieved January 21, 2024, from https://youtu.be/Yel6Wqn4I78?si=_sh_x5R6hl_8XfvX.

Sarah Renae Clark. (2021d). *Controversial Color Theory: RYB vs CMY Color Wheel - What Are the REAL Primary Colors?* YouTube. Retrieved January 21, 2024, from https://youtu.be/yRQmV4XYmqI?si=_XoURFiu6YjM2fz9.

SRV Media. (2023, July 18). *The Science of Colors in Brand Communication: Creating Impactful Brand Identities.* LinkedIn. https://www.linkedin.com/pulse/science-colors-brand-communication-creating-impactful-identities/

Strydom, L. (2018, February 13). *Review: AJR's "Sober Up" Music Video Reveals True Meaning.* The Red & Black. https://www.redandblack.com/culture/review-ajr-s-sober-up-music-video-reveals-true-meaning/article_82e97fb0-1078-11e8-a076-af4978704134.html

The Color Wheel Company. (2023, June). *Color Wheel: A Guide to Mixing Color.* https://colorwheelco.com/

The University of Waikato. (n.d.). *Light Wavelengths.* Science Learning Hub. sciencelearn.org.nz

Tursucular, A. (n.d.). *What Is HSB/HSV?* https://alitursucular.github.io/color-codes-conversion-website-demo/what-is-hsb-hsv.html

Digital Color Tools

- *Adobe Color* | Color.Adobe.com | https://color.adobe.com/create/color-wheel
- *CMYK Colors: CMYK Calculator* | W3Schools.com | https://www.W3Schools.com/colors/colors_cmyk.asp
- *CMYK to Pantone - Color Converter. Find PMS Colors Close to CMYK Color* | https://www.ginifab.com/feeds/pms/cmyk_to_pantone.php
- *Colour Contrast Checker by W. Tarpey* | https://colourcontrast.cc/
- *HTML Color Picker* | W3Schools.com | https://www.w3schools.com/colors/colors_picker.asp
- *RGB Color Codes Chart* | RapidTables.com https://www.rapidtables.com/web/color/RGB_Color.html
- *Pantone* | https://www.Pantone.com/
- *Who Can Use* | https://www.whocanuse.com/

References for Part Two | Autism Spectrum Disorder

Accommodations. *Disability Resources for Students.* (n.d.). https://depts.washington.edu/uwdrs/current-students/accommodations/

Autistic Self Advocacy Network (ASAN). (2021, December 9). *Functioning Labels Harm Autistic People.* https://autisticadvocacy.org/2021/12/functioning-labels-harm-autistic-people/

Autistic Women+ Living Authentically (AW+ LA) Facebook Group.

Baker, G. (2021). *Rainbow Warrior: My Life in Color.* Chicago Review Press.

Baldani, S. (n.d.). *Turning Vibration and Rhythm into Extraordinary Images.* City Lifestyle. https://citylifestyle.com/articles/turning-vibration-and-rhythm-into-extraordinary-images

Bargiela, S., Steward, R., & Mandy, W. (2016, October). *The Experiences of Late-diagnosed Women with Autism Spectrum Conditions: An Investigation of the Female Autism Phenotype.* Journal of Autism and Developmental Disorders. https://www.ncbi.nlm.nih.gov/pmc/

articles/PMC5040731/?fbclid=IwAR3a8CfDYOOQZSJft2defdIwJTmiud9LJAQ-B8DQXLyUViEYYLJsHmFx6QI#CR10

Benham, J. L., & Kizer, J. S. (2016). *Aut-ors of Our Experience: Interrogating Intersections of Autistic Identity*. Canadian Journal of Disability Studies, 5(3), 77–113. https://doi.org/10.15353/cjds.v5i3.298

Blanchfield, A.T. (2023, May 8). *How a Glimmer Triggers Feelings of Joy and Safety*. Verywell Mind. https://www.verywellmind.com/what-is-a-glimmer-5323168#:~:text=Triggers%20are%20cues%E2%80%94accurate%20or,into%20the%20ventral%20vagal%20state.

Boissonnault, W. G. (2005). *Primary Care for the Physical Therapist: Examination and Triage* (1st ed.). Elsevier/Saunders.

Brabban, A. & Turkington, D. (2002) *The Search for Meaning: Detecting Congruence Between Life Events, Underlying Schema and Psychotic Symptoms*. In A.P. Morrison (Ed) A Casebook of Cognitive Therapy for Psychosis (Chap 5, p59-75). New York: Brunner-Routledge.

Burgess, R. (2022, March 30). *Understanding the Spectrum—A Comic Strip Explanation*. The Art of Autism. https://the-art-of-autism.com/understanding-the-spectrum-a-comic-strip-explanation/

Captain Quirk., (2021, October 11). *We Need to Stop Saying "We're All a Little Autistic."* Autistic Not Weird. https://autisticnotweird.com/stop-saying/

Diagnostic and Statistical Manual of Mental Disorders: DSM-5. (5th ed.). (2013). American Psychiatric Association.

Elsherif, M. M., Middleton, S. L., Phan, J. M., Azevedo, F., Iley, B. J., Grose-Hodge, M., ... Dokovova, M. (2022, June 20). *Bridging Neurodiversity and Open Scholarship: How Shared Values Can Guide Best Practices for Research Integrity, Social Justice, and Principled Education*. https://doi.org/10.31222/osf.io/k7a9p

Engelbrecht, N., & Silvertant, E. (2024, January 25). *The Ultimate Autism Resource*. Embrace Autism. https://embrace-autism.com/

Exclusive Says. (n.d.). *What Is Autism? A Simple Guide to Understanding the Spectrum.* Exclusive Says. https://exclusive.says.com/my/exclusive/what-is-autism-a-simple-guide-to-understanding-the-spectrum/

Flowers, J., Dawes, J., McCleary, D., & Marzolf, H. (2023). *Words Matter: Language Preferences in a Sample of Autistic Adults.* Neurodiversity, 1, 1-11. https://doi.org/10.1177/27546330231216548

Gage, C. (2024). *The Delilah Journal: Reflections on Being Diagnosed Extremely Late in Life As Autistic.* Lulu.com.

Grosso, J. (2022). *Make your Day.* TikTok. https://www.tiktok.com/@heydrjustine/video/7063830906879986991

Heyworth, M. (2024, February 16). *Introduction to Autism, Part 1: What Is Autism?* Reframing Autism. https://reframingautism.org.au/introduction-to-autism-part-1-what-is-autism/

Hull, L., Petrides, K. V., Allison, C., Smith, P., Baron-Cohen, S., Lai, M.-C., & Mandy, W. (2017). *"Putting on My Best Normal": Social Camouflaging in Adults with Autism Spectrum Conditions.* Journal of Autism and Developmental Disorders, 47(8), 2519–2534. https://doi.org/10.1007/s10803-017-3166-5

Jack, C. (n.d.). *ATAA Autism Wheel.* Autistic Awareness with Claire Jack, PhD. https://www.facebook.com/drclairejack/

Karanzalis, L. (2019, December 5). *Executive Functioning - ADDvantages Learning Center: South Jersey.* ADDvantages Learning Center | South Jersey. https://addvantageslearningcenter.com/executive-functioning/

Keating, C. T., Hickman, L. Leung, J., Monk, R., Montgomery, A., Heath, H., & Sowden, S. (2022). *Autism-related Language Preferences of English-speaking Individuals Across the Globe: A Mixed Methods Investigation.* Autism Research, 16(2), 245-473. https://doi.org/10.1002/aur.2864

Kotowicz, A. (2022). *What I Mean When I Say I'm Autistic: Unpuzzling a Life on the Autism Spectrum.* Neurobeautiful.

Lynch, C. L., & C.L. Lynch (2022, May 23). *"Autism Is a Spectrum" Doesn't Mean What You Think.* NeuroClastic. https://neuroclastic.com/its-a-spectrum-doesnt-mean-what-you-think/

Marschall, Amy P. (2022, December 9). *Who Can Diagnose Autism in Adults?* Verywell Mind. https://www.verywellmind.com/who-can-diagnose-autism-in-adults-6748943#:~:text=A%20psychologist%20or%20a%20psychiatrist%20completes%20an%20evaluation%20if%20they,in%20psychological%20assessments%20and%20autism.

May, M. P., Kiss, I. G., & Carter, A. S. (2016). *Definitions and Classification of Autism Spectrum Disorders.* In Stone-MacDonald, D. F., Cihak, & D. Zager (Eds.), Autism Spectrum Disorders: Identification, Education, and Treatment (pp. 1-22). Taylor & Francis. https://doi.org/10.4324/9781315794181

Mazefsky CA, Herrington J, Siegel M, et al. *The Role of Emotion Regulation in Autism Spectrum Disorder.* J Am Acad Child Adolesc Psychiatry. 2013;52(7):679–688. doi:10.1016/j.jaac.2013.05.006

Mcleod, S. (2024, January 24). *Maslow's Hierarchy of Needs.* Simply Psychology. https://www.simplypsychology.org/maslow.html

Middleton S., Iley, B., Sulik, J., Elsherif, M. E., Azevedo, F. (2024). *The Academic Wheel of Privilege: An Equity-based Tool for Authorship Order.* https://forrt.org/publications/

Milner, V., McIntosh, H., Colvert, E., & Happé, F. (2019). *A Qualitative Exploration of the Female Experience of Autism Spectrum Disorder (ASD).* Journal of Autism and Developmental Disorders, 49(6), 2389–2402. https://doi.org/10.1007/s10803-019-03906-4

Murray, F. (Feb 28, 2023). *We Need to Talk about Aspie Supremacists. Thinking Person's Guide to Autism.* https://thinkingautismguide.com/2023/02/we-need-to-talk-about-aspie-supremacists.html

National Alliance to End Homelessness. (2024, January 6). State of Homelessness: 2023 Edition. https://endhomelessness.org/homelessness-in-america/homelessness-statistics/state-of-homelessness/

Neff, M. A. (2024, January 18). *Autistic Burnout Symptoms. Insights of a Neurodivergent Clinician.* https://neurodivergentinsights.com/blog/autistic-burnout-symptoms

Neff, M. A. (2023b, September 17). *How to Use Pacing Systems. Insights of a Neurodivergent Clinician.* https://neurodivergentinsights.com/blog/how-to-use-pacing-systems

Neff, M. A. (2023, September 8). *Neurodivergent Spoon Theory. Insights of a Neurodivergent Clinician.* https://neurodivergentinsights.com/blog/the-neurodivergent-spoon-drawer-spoon-theory-for-adhders-and-autists

Neuroscience News. (2021, September 27). *Number Diagnosed with Autism Jumps 787 Percent in Two Decades.* Neuroscience News. Retrieved February 4, 2023, from https://neurosciencenews.com/austim-rate-increase-19368/

Nicolaidis, C., Raymaker, D. M., Ashkenazy, E., McDonald, K. E., Dern, S., Baggs, A. E. V., Kapp, S. K., Weiner, M., & Boisclair, W. C. (2015). *"Respect the Way I Need to Communicate With You": Healthcare Experiences of Adults on the Autism Spectrum.* Autism, 19(7), 824–831. https://doi.org/10.1177/1362361315576221

Neo, P. (2023, June 24). *Tired of Triggers? Seek out Glimmers to Inspire & Nourish Instead.* mindbodygreen RSS. https://www.mindbodygreen.com/articles/what-are-glimmers

Pearson, A. & Rose, K. (2021). *A Conceptual Analysis of Autistic Masking: Understanding the Narrative of Stigma and the Illusion of Choice.* Autism in Adulthood, 3(1), 52-60. http://doi.org/10.1089/aut.2020.0043

Pew Research Center. (2021, November 9). *Beyond Red vs. Blue: The Political Typology.* Pew Research Center - U.S. Politics & Policy. https://www.pewresearch.org/politics/2021/11/09/beyond-red-vs-blue-the-political-typology-2/

Ponte, K. (2022, January 10). *Understanding Mental Illness Triggers.* NAMI. https://www.nami.org/Blogs/NAMI-Blog/January-2022/Understanding-Mental-Illness-Triggers

Porges, S. W., & Dana, D. (2018). *Clinical Applications of the Polyvagal Theory: The Emergence of Polyvagal-informed Therapies.* W.W. Norton & Company, Inc.

Price, D. (2022). *Unmasking Autism: Discovering the New Faces of Neurodiversity* (First edition.). Harmony Books.

Price, D. (2019, August 14). *From Self-diagnosis to Self-realization.* Medium. https://devonprice.medium.com/from-self-diagnosis-to-self-realization-852e3a069451

Raymaker, D. M., Teo, A. R., Steckler, N. A., Lentz, B., Scharer, M., Delos Santos, A., Kapp, S. K., Hunter, M., Joyce, A., & Nicolaidis, C. (2020*). "Having All of Your Internal Resources Exhausted Beyond Measure and Being Left with No Clean-up Crew": Defining Autistic Burnout.* Autism in Adulthood, 2(2), 132–143. https://doi.org/10.1089/aut.2019.0079

Reframing Autism. (n.d.) *Information Archives.* https://reframingautism.org.au/category/information/

Rivera, L. (2023, June 16). *Asking Autistics: What Do You Wish Non-Autistics Understood About Autism and Autistic People?* Neurodivergent Rebel. https://neurodivergentrebel.com/2023/06/16/askingautistics-what-do-you-wish-non-autistics-understood-about-autism-and-autistic-people/

Sandin, S., Lichtenstein, P., Kuja-Halkola, R., Hultman, C., Larsson, H., & Reichenberg, A. (2017). *The Heritability of Autism Spectrum Disorder.* JAMA, 318(12), 1182–1184. https://doi.org/10.1001%2Fjama.2017.12141

Sheffer, E. (2018). *Asperger's Children: The Origins of Autism in Nazi Vienna.* W. W. Norton and Company.

Taboas, A., Doepke, K., & Zimmerman, C. (2023). *Preferences for Identity-first Versus Person-first Language in a US Sample of Autism Stakeholders.* Autism, 27, 565–570. https://doi.org/10.1177/13623613221130845

The University of North Carolina at Chapel Hill. (2022, May 23*). Understanding Mental Health Triggers.* Campus Health. https://campushealth.unc.edu/health-topic/understanding-mental-health-triggers/#:~:text=A%20 trigger%20is%20a%20stimulus,%2C%20and%2For%20eating%20disorders

Tuxford-Adams, L. (2024, March). Personal communication. Neurokindred. Queensland, Australia.

UCLA Health. (2023, October 12). *Understanding Undiagnosed Autism in Adult Females.* UCLA Health. https://www.uclahealth.org/news/understanding-undiagnosed-autism-adult-females#:~:text=But%20experts%20are%20realizing%20that,never%20been%20able%20to%20explain.

Walker, N. (2022, July 19). *Neurodiversity: Some Basic Terms & Definitions.* Neuroqueer. https://neuroqueer.com/neurodiversity-terms-and-definitions/

Warrier, V., Greenberg, D.M., Weir, E., Buckingham, C., Smith, P., Lai, M. C., Allison, C., & Baron-Cohen, S. (2020). *Elevated Rates of Autism, Other Neurodevelopmental and Psychiatric Diagnoses, and Autistic Traits in Transgender and Gender-diverse Individuals.* Nature Communications, 11, Article 3959. https://doi.org/10.1038/s41467-020-17794-1

Weller, G. (2023, October 16). *A is for Autism, but a Capital A is Even Better.* The Unmasked Autistic. https://theunmaskedautistic.com/a-is-for-autism-but-a-capital-a-is-even-better/

Wise, S.J. (n.d.). *Resources.* Lived Experience Educator. https://www.livedexperienceeducator.com/resources

Appendix A. Color Models Quick Reference Guide

The guide continues on the next page.

Subtractive Primaries		Additive Primaries
Mixing of Colorants		Mixing of Light
Light is reflected from an object You see what is reflected 👁 You don't see what is absorbed 🚫👁		Light is from a light source
Main application: paints, dyes, inks	Main application: printing plus paints, dyes, inks	Application: digital
Artist's Primaries / Traditional Primaries Red, Yellow, Blue (RYB)	**Printer's Primaries / Modern Primaries** Cyan, Magenta, Yellow (CMY), Black (CMYK)	**Additive Primaries** Red, Green, Blue (RGB)
Artist's Secondaries Orange, Green, Violet (OGV)	**Printer's Secondaries** Red, Blue, Green (RBG)	**Additive Secondaries** Cyan, Magenta, Yellow (CMY)
Color Wheel	Mixing Wheel	LED Light Mixing (RGB) Red: R (100%) G (0%) B (0%) Green: R (0%) G (100%) B (0%) Blue: R (0%) G (0%) B (100%) Magenta: R (100%) G (0%) B (100%) Yellow: R (100%) G (100%) B (0%) Cyan: R (0%) G (100%) B (100%) White: RGB (100% each)

Appendix B. HEX Code Explanation

HEX code writes 1–9 as two digits:
00, 01, 02, 03, 04, 05, 06, 07, 08, 09

And then introduces six letters (A–F) to represent 10 – 15:
10=A, 11=B, 12=C, 13=D, 14=E, 15=F

Then, standard counting (10–19) picks up from where the 0–9 left off.
16=10, 17=11, 18=12, 19=13, 20=14, 21=15, 22=16, 23=17, 24=18, 25=19

Similar to how the counting changed at "09," it also shifts at 19 and is written as "1" + (letters A–F):
26=1A, 27=1B, 28=1C, 29=1D, 30=1E, 31=1F

This pattern continues and repeats until 255. Here's the complete key:

00, 01, 02, 03, 04, 05, 06, 07, 08, 09
10=A, 11=B, 12=C, 13=D, 14=E, 15=F,
16=10, 17=11, 18=12, 19=13, 20=14, 21=15, 22=16, 23=17, 24=18, 25=19,
26=1A, 27=1B, 28=1C, 29=1D, 30=1E, 31=1F
32=20, 33=21, 34=22, 35=23, 36=24, 37=25, 38=26, 39=27, 40=28, 41=29
42=2A, 43=2B, 44=2C, 45=2D, 46=2E, 47=2F
48=30, 49=31, 50=32, 51=33, 52=34, 53=35, 54=36, 55=37, 56=38, 57=39
58=3A, 59=3B, 60=3C, 61=3D, 62=3E, 63=3F

64=40, 65=41, 66=42, 67=43, 68=44, 69=45, 70=46, 71=47, 72=48, 73=49
74=4A ,75=4B, 76=4C, 77=4D, 78=4E, 79=4F
80=50, 81=51, 82=52, 83=53, 84=54, 85=55, 86=56, 87=57, 88=58, 89=59,
90=5A, 91=5B, 92=5C, 93=5D, 94=5E, 95=5F
96=60, 97=61, 98=62, 99=63, 100=64, 101=65, 102=66, 103=67, 104=68, 105=69
106=6A, 107=6B, 108=6C, 109=6D, 110=6E, 111=6F
112=70, 113=71, 114=72, 115=73, 116=74, 117=75, 118=76, 119=77, 120=78, 121=79
122=7A, 123=7B, 124=7C, 125=7D, 126=7E, 127=7F
128=80, 129=81, 130=82, 131=83, 132=84, 133=85, 134=86, 135=87, 136=88, 137=89
138=8A, 139=8B, 140=8C, 141=8D, 142=8E, 143=8F
144=90, 145=91, 146=92, 147=93, 148=94, 149=95, 150=96, 151=97, 152=98, 153=99
154=9A, 155=9B, 156=9C, 157=9D, 158=9E, 159=9F
160=A0, 161=A1, 162=A2, 163=A3, 164=A4, 165=A5, 166=A6, 167=A7, 168=A8, 169=A9
170=AA, 171=AB, 172=AC, 173=AD, 174=AE, 175=AF
176=B0, 177=B1, 178=B2, 179=B3, 180=B4, 181=B5, 182=B6, 183=B7, 184=B8, 185=B9
186=BA, 187=BB, 188=BC, 189=BD, 190=BE, 191=BF
192=C0, 193=C1, 194=C2, 195=C3, 196=C4, 197=C5, 198=C6, 199=C7, 200=C8, 201=C9
202=CA, 203=CB, 204=CC, 205=CD, 206=CE, 207=CF
208=D0, 209=D1, 210=D2, 211=D3, 212=D4, 213=D5, 214=D6, 215=D7, 216=D8, 217=D9
218=DA, 219=DB, 220=DC, 221=DD, 222=DE, 223=DF
224=E0, 225=E1, 226=E2, 227=E3, 228=E4, 229=E5, 230=E6, 231=E7, 232=E8, 233=E9
234=EA, 235=EB, 236=EC, 237=ED, 238=EE, 239=EF
240=F0, 241=F1, 242=F2, 243=F3, 244=F4, 245=F5, 246=F6, 247=F7, 248=F8, 249=F9
250=FA, 251=FB, 252=FC, 253=FD, 254=FE, 255=FF

Acknowledgements

My sincere gratitude to anyone who has crossed my path along my journey. Every touch point matters.

To my daughters, Ellie and Grace. Thank you both for sharing your graphic expertise with me and other *confetti dreamers*.

To my therapists, Emily and Krista, thank you for taking the time to get to know me. You were instrumental in helping me learn how to embrace my authentic self.

To Dr. Kelly Bruhn and Professor Jill Van Wyke at Drake University, your feedback and guidance throughout the Master of Communication program helped me create my business plan and communication strategy for Confetti Dreamers. Thank you for helping Drake students fulfill their dreams. Go bulldogs!

To Chandler Bolt, founder of Selfpublishing.com, your mission to help others make a difference through writing and publishing a book is admirable, yet personal. You are making Kendall proud, one book at a time. I have been blessed to collaborate with your amazing team. A special call out to:

- Coaches Andrew, Allison, and Brittany
- Qatarina's amazing editing team, including chief editor Katelynn
- The incredible book production team, including Dakota, Jude, Honeylette, and Sofia.

I am beyond blessed to have found the Facebook group Autistic Women+ Living Authentically. A special thanks to everyone who participated in my research in 2023. An extra dose of gratitude to Linda, Sandra Kay, and Mia for your roles.

And, finally, a special callout to:

Linda Tuxford-Adams (Queensland, Australia) for sharing her Autism expertise. Please visit her wonderful website for her non-profit Neurokindred: Counselling and Peer Support for Thriving Autistically (http://neurokindred.com).

Neil Ward (Des Moines, Iowa, USA) for sharing his color expertise. Check out Neil O. Ward (https://neiloward.com) to see his cool mid-century silk screen designs, prints, and more.

Spread the News!

Thank you so much for reading my book!

If you enjoyed reading this book as much as I enjoyed researching and writing it, would you be so kind as to leave me a review? My goal is to spread the word about neurodiversity and Autism, and your voice matters!

My hope is for others to experience the peace that comes with living authentically—sooner than later.

I would love to hear from you! What resonated with you? What inspired you? What would you like more of?

Your feedback will help me and other readers on our quest for authenticity.

Please take a few minutes to leave a helpful review on Amazon:

confettidreamers.com/review

Eternally grateful,

~ Shannon Hilscher

Check Out My Other Book

An Adventure into Our Colored World: The Before and After

I started my color journey when I wrote *The Unexpected Adventure That Changed My World* with the intention of modeling figurative language to convey colorful imagery while integrating the science of color. I finished my rough draft in 2020 while feeling frustrated by the massively divided political climate in the United States of America. After attending *Hamilton*, the hit musical, I became obsessed with its soundtrack. I wrote furiously while cranking up the volume to songs like "My Shot," motivating me to finish what was morphing into an allegory with themes of diversity, equity, inclusion, and belonging (DEIB). The finished product is a feel-good book with easy integrations into thematic teaching—language arts, science, DEIB, and more—for readers at the 5th-grade reading level and up. Together, let's embrace our colors and uniqueness to better our world.

Public Service Announcement (PSA)

For those of you in the United States, the progress of our nation is at risk.

Please take a moment to think about what is important to you:

- The right to freedom.
- The right to be your authentic self.
- The right to vote.
- The right to make decisions about your body.
- The right to safety.
- The right to accurate information and news.

Again, your voice really does matter! Please vote.

To learn more, please look for unbiased sources to learn about politicians, such as National Public Radio (https://www.npr.org/) (NPR).

Spread the word. Take time to cast your vote.

Thank you.

Index

Accommodations, 152, 155
academic, 156
workplace, 112, 156
Adaptive Therapy for Autistic Adults (ATAA®) Autism Wheel©, 117
ADHD, 122, 127, 148, 163
co-occurring diagnoses, 148
Asperger's Disorder, 110
Aura, 167-168
authentic self, 103, 131, 155, 162, 168
Autism Spectrum Disorder (ASD), 108, 110, 118-119, 151, 154, 156, 160
diagnosis, 149, 152
effects, 149
levels, 118
reactions to, 157
seek a diagnosis of ASD, 149-150
traits, 120
visual representations of, 113-118
Autism, undiagnosed, 112-113, 151

Autistic people
learn from, 111 See options for seeking ASD diagnosis
Autistic Women+ Living Authentically, 111, 137, 141, 147, 159
Autistic women+, 110-112
Belonging, 164-165 See also Maslow's Hierarchy of Needs
Biv, Roy G., 58-59
Black, 21-22, 39, 47-49, 80, 90, 95
Brown, 23-24, 92
Burnout, 127, 130, 162
Camouflaging, 112, 148
Clinical diagnosis, 150, 157
pros and cons of, 152
Clinical evaluations, reactions to, 154
CMY Color Wheel, 41-42
CMY Venn Diagram, 62
CMYK Calculator, 45
CMYK for printing, 44
cognitive distortions, 139, 157
color

achromatic, 29
analogous, 31, 57, 31, 52
as special interest, 1, 142
blindness, 5
complementary, 32, 53, 62
formulas, 28, 51, 167
monochromatic, 30, 132
split-complementary, 33, 54
tetrad, 35, 56
triad, 34, 55
using, 36
Color meanings, 78, 83
cultural, 94-95
Color models, 8, 68
Color pickers, 72
Color psychology, 78-79, 93
Color story, 78-79
Color theory, 13, 44, 75, 78
Color timeline, 10
Colorants. See pigments and dyes
Compassion, 97, 111
Confetti Dreamers, 76, 80-81, 126
Coping
emotion-focused, 136
make a plan, 135
problem-focused 135
Reflect, 134
with stress, 124
Creativity, 36, 81
DELILAA, 158
De-stressor, 132
Diagnosis rates, 112
Diagnostic and Statistical
    Manual of Mental
    Disorders (DSM), 106
Digital colors, 68
Digital file formats, 74
DSM- 5, 110, 148
Dyes, 9-10

Dyspraxia, 120, 122
Education, 109, 112, 138, 155
Empathy, 111, 123, 148
Equal parts, 20, 61
Esteem, 165 See also Maslow's
    Hierarchy of Needs
Everyone's Autistic, 119
Executive functioning, 126-128
Formal diagnosis. See
    clinical diagnosis
Glimmers, 134
Gray Scale & Value Finder, 18
Gray, 19, 23, 68, 91
Harmonious, 28, 51
HEX codes, 66-68
Hue, 17, 43, 68-71
complementary, 53
Imposter syndrome, 103, 135, 155
Inclusivity, 97, 111
Inspired, 81
Intensity, 17-18
Language, identity-first, 110
Light source, 4
Love and belonging, 164
Masking, 112-113, 153, 163
Maslow's Hierarchy of Needs,
    104, 161-162
Meltdown, 127-128, 137, 149
Modern primaries (CMY), 39
Neurodivergent, 106-107, 129
    traits, 113
Neurodiversity, 99, 101, 105, 150
spectrums of, 107
Neurotypical, 106-107, 112, 152
Neutral gray, 19, 23
Neutralizer, 25
Next steps, 121
Official diagnosis see
    clinical diagnosis

Orthogonality, 102
Pacing, 142, 144
Pantone Matching
    System (PMS), 76
Passion, 155, 171
Photoreceptors, 4-5
Physiological needs, 162 See also
    Maslow's Hierarchy of Needs
Pigments, 8-10
Primary colors, 11, 16, 38, 43, 59
additive, 7, 59, 61
subtractive, 7, 11, 38
Printer's primaries, 7, 44, 190
Printing, 74, 76
Quirky, 81, 103
Rainbows, 96-97
Resources, 111-112, 127, 145, 163
diagnostic, 150
employment-related, 164
RGB Venn Diagram, 61
RYB color wheel, 14-15
RYB Venn Diagram, 16
Safety needs, 163
Safety, 163-164 See also Maslow's
    Hierarchy of Needs
Secondary colors, 16, 40, 60
Self-actualization, 166 See also
    Maslow's Hierarchy of Needs
Self-care, 141-142, 145
Self-diagnosis, 150
controversy, 151
pros and cons of, 152
Self-discovery, 147, 157
Self-identification, 150
pros and cons, 152
Self-realization, 150, 156 See
    options for seeking
    ASD diagnosis

Sensory overload, 126-
    129, 156, 163
Shades, 18, 30
Shutdown, 127-128
Skin tones, 24-26
Spectrum, 154
Spoons, 129
Stimming, 142-143
Stimuli, 109, 132
Stress bucket, 128
Stress, 124
    color of, 125
    coping with, 132, 134
    emotional, 164
Synesthesia, 123
Temperature, 17, 19
Tertiary colors, 16, 43
Tints, 18
Tones, 18
Traditional primaries
    (RYB), 7, 11, 38
Traits, 93, 121-122
autistic, 119-120, 146, 158
neurodivergent, 113
Trigger warnings, 137-138
Triggers, 128, 14
coping 134
True colors, 105, 167
Value, 18, 43, 70
White light, 61-62
White, 22

www.ingramcontent.com/pod-product-compliance
Lightning Source LLC
Chambersburg PA
CBHW061735070526
44585CB00024B/2677

9 781734 607437